MW01634076

Spies, Scoundrels and Rogues of the Ohio Frontier

Gary S. Williams

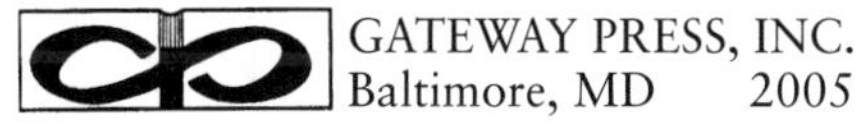

GATEWAY PRESS, INC.
Baltimore, MD   2005

Copyright © 2005 by
Gary S. Williams
All rights reserved.

Permission to reproduce in any form
must be secured from the author.

Photos by Owen Williams

Please direct all correspondence and book orders to:
Gary S. Williams
42100 Williams Lane
Caldwell, OH 43724
Phone: (740) 732-8169 or (740) 732-7291
Email: buckeye_books@earthlink.net
Web site: www.buckeyebookpress.com

Library of Congress Control Number 2005921031
ISBN: 0-9703395-2-6

Published for the author by
Gateway Press, Inc.
1001 N. Calvert Street
Baltimore, MD 21202-3897

www.gatewaypress.com

Printed in the United States of America

Cover photo: The Ohio River from Monroe County, Ohio
Cover design by: Kate Boyer

TABLE OF CONTENTS

INTRODUCTION

The land between the Great Lakes and the states bordering the Ohio River is quintessentially American today. Yet for a 60-year period the fate of this area was up for grabs. Those vying for control of this resource rich region between 1754 and 1814 included England, France, Spain, the United States, several private schemers, and of course the various native tribes that were the original inhabitants.

The first half of this period saw the defeat of France and then England. In the next 30 years the area became the first great test for the new American republic. Ohio was the first place settled by free Americans with constitutionally guaranteed civil liberties, but this experiment was by no means assured of success. With England still maintaining forts on the Great Lakes and Spain controlling the mouth of the Mississippi, the Indians still had European allies who shared an interest in limiting American expansion.

With so much at stake, there was a considerable potential for side-switching and intrigue. The story of the eventual success of the United States has been told through the lives of many frontier heroes, but this era of shifting alliances was also full of fascinating characters of more questionable repute. Among the examples profiled here are:

. a famous soldier and author who failed in his attempt to create a transcontinental empire and died in disgrace

. a Tory spy who originally impressed George Washington but wound up alienating everyone with his lies and bullying

. the most famous and most hated of renegade traitors

. two ill-suited officers who led Americans into massacres

- a popular folk legend who lived to kill Indians
- the most notorious organized crime figure of the frontier
-an Indian Agent who betrayed Indians and whites alike in both times of peace and war, yet died a hero's death
-the only one of the Burr Conspirators to escape unscathed, although he was more guilty than any of them

These subjects range chronologically from accused traitors Robert Rogers to Aaron Burr, and in public estimation from Lewis Wetzel to Simon Girty. In the underpopulated world of the frontier, many of them knew each other as well as the significant heroes of the era.

To label someone a spy, scoundrel or rogue implies passing judgment, but these portraits are meant to be at least balanced, if not sympathetic. All of the subjects portrayed had to have possessed considerable skills in order to rise to a position of prominence where they could do some damage. While many of them earned their labels by the sides they chose and how and why they chose them, some achieved distinction by exercising questionable judgment on behalf of the United States. Presented here in chronological order, their behavior collectively tells the story of a colorful era of international intrigue centered in the heartland of present day America.

This book is not a scholarly study. There are no footnotes and it has mostly been researched through secondary sources. But the stories that follow are all true ones. When an absence of facts has made it necessary to include unverified legends, they are labeled as such. The real stories of these flawed people whose fascinating behavior helped shape the fate of the new nation are as much a part of history as the stories of our heroes.

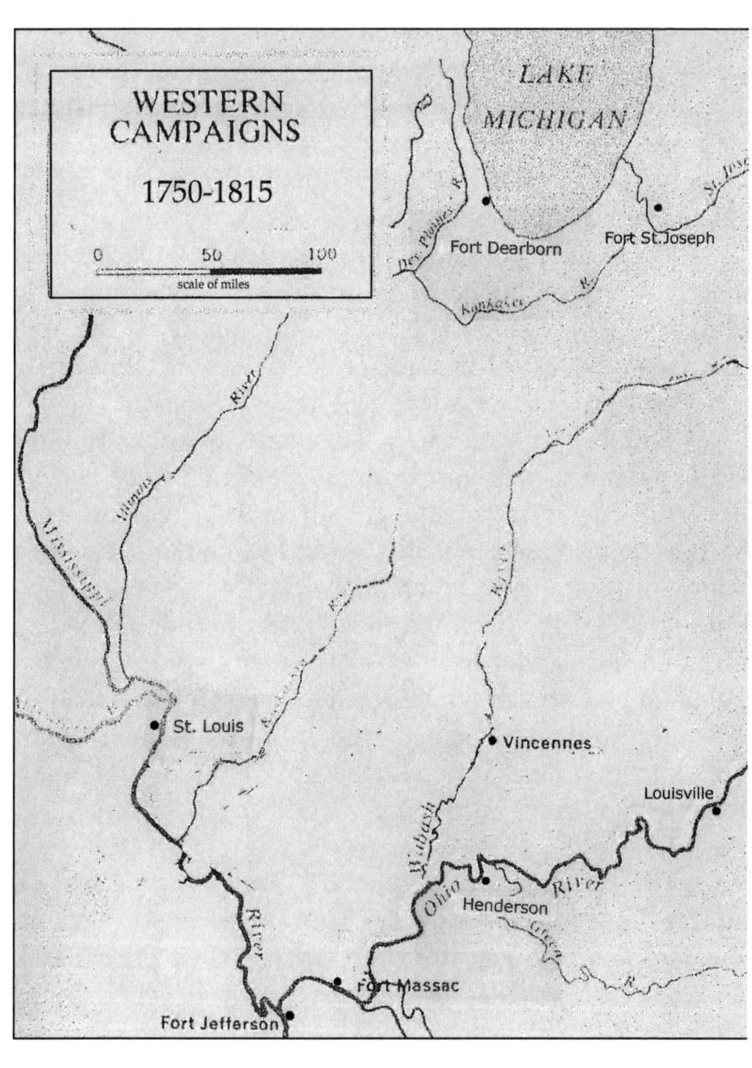

WESTERN CAMPAIGNS
1750-1815
0   50   100
scale of miles
LAKE MICHIGAN
Des Plaines R.
Kankakee R.
St. Joseph
Fort Dearborn
Fort St. Joseph
Mississippi
Illinois River
St. Louis
Vincennes
Louisville
Wabash
Ohio
River
Henderson
Green R.
Fort Massac
Fort Jefferson

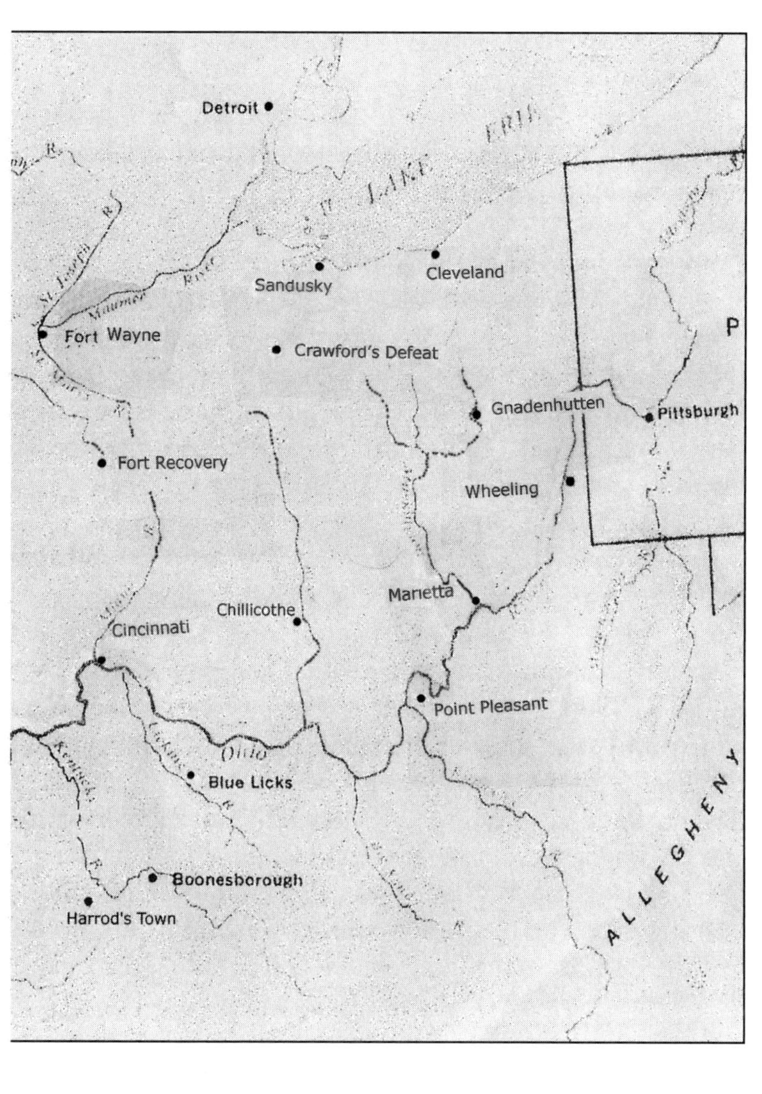

Detroit
LAKE ERIE
Sandusky
Cleveland
Fort Wayne
Crawford's Defeat
Gnadenhutten
Pittsburgh
Fort Recovery
Wheeling
Marietta
Chillicothe
Cincinnati
Point Pleasant
Ohio
Blue Licks
Boonesborough
Harrod's Town
Kentucky
Maumee River
St. Joseph R.
St. Mary's R.
P
ALLEGHENY

ACKNOWLEDGMENTS

There is too much involved in production for any book to be said to be self-published, and a lot of help from many people went into this one. Ideas for chapters came from Richard Michael, who nominated Samuel Mason, and from Barb Meiring of the Fort Recovery Museum, who first suggested William Wells. Joseph Bonamico, who portrays Simon Girty on stage, was very generous with his help on that chapter, and Ray Swick of Blennerhassett Island Historical State Park offered insight on the chapter on the Burr Conspirators. Librarians everywhere were helpful as always, with particular thanks going to Rebecca Poe of Marietta College Special Collections, Andrew Whitis of Muskingum College, and Terry Mullins, who compiled the index.

Closer to home, my family offered all kinds of essential support. Foremost in this category was my wife Mary Williams, who lent many attributes, not the least of which was patience. Our daughter Meryl Williams typed the manuscript, and our son Owen Williams was responsible for the illustrations. My brother Brian Williams edited for style and my father Les Williams for content. And my mother, the late Kay Hagloch Williams, was also a presence of sorts. As a writer who enjoyed good stories well told, this book is dedicated to her in the hopes that it achieves that goal.

CHAPTER ONE

Robert Rogers
"The famous Major Rogers"

Few people have had the halves of their lifetime in such contrast as Robert Rogers. In 1763, the 32-year-old Rogers had risen from obscurity to become America's greatest war hero. Lionized on both sides of the Atlantic and newly married to a well-connected wife, he appeared to have an unlimited future. Yet by the time he died in a London slum 32 years later, Rogers had returned to obscurity. Disgraced, divorced, and dissipated, the former hero had been jailed and accused of treason on both sides of the Atlantic. His rise and fall was an American tragedy that he contributed to with his reckless greed and ambition. And his vision of the Northwest Territory played a role in his downfall.

Robert Rogers was born on November 18, 1731 at Methuen, Massachusetts, the fourth of eight children of James and Mary Rogers. His Scots-Irish parents had only recently arrived on the banks of the Merrimack River in the northeastern part of the colony. Like many of their neighbors, they were farmers who came to this country because it offered fresh opportunity and a chance to own their own farm. But the Rogers clan arrived too late, for the best land in Methuen was taken.

In the New England tradition, education was not neglected even on the frontier, and young Robert attended school in Methuen until about the age of eight. But he left schooling forever in 1739 when the family moved to New Hampshire farther upstream on the fertile Merrimack. They purchased an isolated tract ten miles from the nearest town of Rumford, now called Concord.

Living on the edge of civilization, Robert now got a different sort of education. He learned wilderness survival skills and a love and respect for the outdoors. He was also taught the rudiments of farming, but this lesson he did not take to, as he developed a distaste for the drudgery of farm labor.

The outbreak of King George's War in 1744 gave him an early opportunity to escape his farm chores. This was one of a series of wars between England and France that were fought in both Europe and North America. The local manifestation was an increase in French-led Indian raiding parties from Canada on isolated New England settlements. In answering the local military call for defense, Robert Rogers signed on as a fourteen-year-old. His unit saw no combat, but the young man found he liked the camping, traveling and camaraderie of military life.

But there were real dangers in this war, as the family found out in the spring of 1748. Warned of raiding parties in the area, the Rogers clan fled to Rumford for protection. When they returned, they found that their ten years of homesteading had been wiped out. Their house had been burned, their livestock killed, and all but a single fruit tree destroyed. The war ended that year, but the family struggle to rebuild would take longer. James Rogers was still trying to maintain his hold on the family farm when he was mistaken for a bear and shot and killed by a family friend in 1753.

By that time, Robert Rogers was living on his own, having bought a nearby farm. John Stark, a neighbor who would go on to fame in the American Revolution, described Rogers as a young man as "six feet in stature, well proportioned, and one of the most athletic men of his time and well known in all trials of strength and activity among the young men of his vicinity and for miles around." He also had, according to Stark, "great presence of mind, intrepidity, perseverance, and a plausible address."

Rogers signed up for road-building crews where he could travel as in the militia. Otherwise he was stuck with the physical toil and fiscal worries of maintaining a farmstead, and he longed for a shortcut. This got him into legal difficulty when he was accused of counterfeiting in 1755. Actual hard currency was rare on the frontier, and Rogers apparently accepted bills he knew were bogus and put them into circulation. He was saved from possible jail time by renewed hostilities with the French and Indians from Canada.

The previous year a then-unknown militia colonel named George Washington had fired upon a French party in western Pennsylvania and within two years the whole world was at war. This war ultimately gave all of French Canada to England, but to Rogers it meant a chance to stay out of jail. Hearing that troops were needed, he not only enlisted but recruited fifty other men from New Hampshire and Massachusetts.

The battlefront in New England centered around Lake Champlain. Today this lake forms the border between New York and Vermont, but then it was held by France and was the key part to an almost all water route between Montreal and New York City. The British army was busy fighting what was called the Seven Years War in Europe and could not spare many troops for the North American phase. What few regular troops they did send went to Pennsylvania under General Braddock in an unsuccessful attempt to take the Forks of the Ohio (now Pittsburgh) from the French.

This meant that the Lake Champlain front was left to colonial militia, or provincials. The Americans headquartered at Albany were led by a civilian named William Johnson. Born in Ireland in 1715, Johnson had emigrated to New York and become one of the wealthiest and most powerful men on the continent. He started out by shrewdly managing his uncle's extensive upstate land holdings, but the key to his success lay in his rapport with the Indians. Living amongst them and like them to the point of having an Indian mistress, he not only cornered the fur trade but became a power broker who could deliver the strength of the powerful Iroquois league of tribes. Named Superintendent of Indian Affairs by the King, Johnson could make or break a young officer's career. In Rogers' case, he did both.

On August 8th, 1755, Rogers reported to Johnson along with his recruits, who had elected him their captain. Because he had military and backwoods experience, Rogers and his men were sent out on a scouting mission, so they were not present when the Americans defeated the French at the Battle of Lake George on September 8. However, five days later, Johnson sent Rogers and five men on a trip to reconnoiter the French forts round Lake Champlain. He came within sight of the French forts, gathered valuable intelligence, and discovered his true calling was being a scout. His success in such missions drew him more assignments and he got better results even than Johnson's favored Mohawk scouts. Johnson had heard about Rogers' previous legal difficulties, but he had this to say about the officer he called "the most active man in our army"-- "I understand some insinuations have been made to his disadvantage. I believe him to be as brave and as honest a man as any I have equal knowledge of."

European armies normally ceased operations during the winter months, but Rogers remained active despite the harsh New England weather. In January of 1756 he led seventeen men on ice skates up the frozen lake on another successful raid. On another expedition that winter, a comrade became sick and Rogers sent the others back. He and a few others brought their fellow soldier back safely a full day after the rest of the party had returned.

War efforts always need heroes for promotional purposes, and with winter slowdowns every day was a slow news day, so Rogers' stature regularly grew with each raid. Johnson's provincial army had essentially been disbanded and was being replaced by a force of regular British troops and new militia. During this period, Rogers remained as a volunteer.

In the reorganized army, he was given an expanded role. The governor of Massachusetts authorized Rogers to form a special unit of rangers that he was able to select and train. Among the officers he chose to lead his elite corps of experienced woodsmen were future Revolutionary War heroes John Stark and Israel Putnam. The rangers were even given their own uniforms, with unique green jackets and canvas leggings, topped off by a Scotch bonnet.

When Rogers returned to New Hampshire to recruit in April of 1756, he was no longer a criminal fearing punishment but a legitimate war hero. He was even invited to join the Masons by Reverend Arthur Browne, the dour pastor of the most prominent church in Portsmouth. And he eventually held the rank of major and was on an almost equal footing with the regular officers of the British army.

Most British officers expressed disdain for the Americans they fought alongside. General James Wolfe, who later died while successfully taking Quebec from the French, wrote that "the Americans are in general the dirtiest, most contemptible cowardly dogs that you can conceive." But some of the more progressive officers like Colonel Thomas Gage realized that the army could learn from Rogers' stealthy style of wilderness combat. Gage had been at Braddock's disastrous defeat in 1755 and he realized that the British method of standing in formation in their red coats was completely ineffective in the North American woods.

Seeking to co-opt ranger techniques and lessen their dependence on the American ruffians, the British asked Rogers to write a document detailing his methods. This was the beginning of the concept of light infantry, which stressed unencumbered troops moving quickly, and Rogers' writings became the first warfare manual written by an American. In a set of 29 general maxims, Rogers' rules for rangering spelled out the keys to his success. Stressing stealth, vigilance, and daring, Rogers had several specific rules he followed. Rangers were to travel single file, and when camping overnight no fires were allowed. Half the men were to be awake on guard duty at all times and rangers never returned by the same route they'd taken. In case of disaster the rangers were to disperse individually and reconvene at a previously arranged location. Rogers' rules are still relevant today and American Special Forces still use them in basic training.

Of course, a major reason for the success of Rogers' Rangers was that the rangers were already excellent woodsmen to begin with. So the British started sending out officers on ranger expeditions to learn their methods first hand. Captain James Dalyell accompanied Rogers on an active raid and after some brisk fighting commented how Rogers "acted the whole time with great calmness." But Gage found he could not replicate Rogers' success and seemed to resent it. He wrote to British commander Jeffrey Amherst that "Rogers is a good man in his own way, but his schemes are very wild, and he has a new one every day."

To be sure, Rogers' Rangers were not always successful. In January of 1757, a group of rangers encountered a large contingent of French troops and lost 29 of 74 men, with Rogers himself the last man to safely return. But the rangers' costliest encounter was the famous Battle on Snowshoes. On March 13, 1758, Rogers and 180 rangers on snowshoes got near the gates of Fort Ticonderoga and ambushed what they thought was a war party. Instead it was the advance guard of a much larger force and the rangers had to drop back and try to hold off the enemy in fierce fighting. While trying to hold on until they could try to escape at night, the rangers and Rogers personally were urged to surrender by the French. But when one small group of rangers got cut off and did try to surrender, they were tied to trees and hacked to death. At dusk the rangers dispersed, but only 54 made it back safely. Rogers was alleged to have escaped by sliding down a precipice known today as Rogers Rock. He had to leave his green field jacket behind and when the French and Indians found identifying papers they rejoiced that they had killed Rogers. They soon found out otherwise.

The British and Americans were gradually gaining the upper hand in this war. In 1759 they captured Forts Ticonderoga and Crown Point and on September 13 of that year Wolfe captured Quebec. On that same day, Rogers left on his biggest raid. His objective was the Indian town of St. Francis, 150 miles away near the St. Lawrence River. Indian war parties from there had terrorized New England settlements for years, although the incident that allowed Amherst to order Rogers to attack occurred when Indians seized British soldiers who were under a flag of truce.

Rogers led 180 rangers in whaleboats up Lake Champlain. At the northern end of the lake he hid his boats and extra supplies and started cross-country. However, he hadn't gotten far when friendly Indians he'd left to guard the boats caught up to him and told him the French had discovered and destroyed his cache. This meant that the enemy knew he was in the area and had destroyed his escape route. Trapped behind enemy lines, Rogers sent a message back to tell Amherst to send provisions to Fort Number Four on the Connecticut River, "that being the way I should return, if at all."

Rogers had the advantage of knowing what his destination was and he was able to make it to St. Francis undetected. At dawn on October 6, the rangers beat the Indians at their own game and completely surprised and destroyed the village, killing over 200 while only losing one man. The rangers then quickly filled their packs with provisions, although some foolishly gave valuable pack space to looted treasures.

One historian has described the return trip from St. Francis as a "sustained nightmare." Some rangers were caught and killed as they followed their practice of breaking into smaller parties to better flee their outraged pursuers. All the rangers faced starvation, as game was scarce, and one group is alleged to have practiced cannibalism when they came upon a group of comrades who had already been killed.

Rogers was in the vanguard this time, but was shocked to find the supplies he desperately needed had just been evacuated from along the Connecticut River. Apparently when the rangers fired their guns to alert the troops waiting with provisions, the latter had panicked and left. Too weak to follow, the devastated rangers faced starvation. But Rogers and a few men with some strength left proceeded to build a raft to float down the Connecticut to the nearest post. This raft was destroyed in rapids, but Rogers summoned the strength to build another, lashing logs together with vines, and made it to Number Four on October 31. A rescue party was sent out immediately and ultimately all but 50 of the rangers made it back.

The next year, the British and Americans captured Montreal, the last remaining major French outpost. However, there were still several isolated French forts in the Great Lakes region. General Amherst felt that the English negotiating position would be enhanced if these outposts could be occupied before winter. He needed someone to take French surrender notifications to these forts as soon as possible and he chose Rogers for this mission.

On September 13, 1760, exactly one year after leaving on the St. Francis raid, Rogers left Montreal leading 200 rangers in whaleboats. This was to be the first English-speaking military mission to enter what is now Ohio. And while previous rangers missions had always departed in the dead of the night, this peace-related force set out at noon. The rangers followed the St. Lawrence to Lake Ontario and portaged at Niagara Falls to Lake Erie. On October 16, they arrived at Fort Presqu' Isle, recently taken from the French, at the present site of Erie, Pennsylvania.

Here Rogers left alone on a side trip to Fort Pitt. He returned with troops who were to form an interim garrison for the French fort at Detroit, and with fur trader George Croghan, an associate of Johnson's who was to help in Indian negotiations. On November 4, the entire group moved on. Not long after entering what is now Ohio the next day, the group was hailed by an Indian hunting party on shore. Members of the Ottawa tribe, they were curious to know the purpose of so large an expedition. It was a potentially tense situation, but the Indians seemed to accept that their French allies had surrendered, and the rangers moved on, although they were similarly questioned on the Marblehead Peninsula and at the mouth of the Detroit River.

This was the first time Rogers had left New England, and he was greatly impressed by what he saw of the northwest. He wrote that "the land on the south side of Lake Erie from Presqu' Isle puts on a very fine appearance. The country level, the timber tall and of the best sort.... it is well watered and for game, both as to plenty and varieties perhaps exceeded by no part of the world."

Rogers encountered storms on Lake Erie and also had to wait at the present site of Port Clinton while final negotiations were made with the French. On November 29, the rangers finally entered Detroit and a transfer ceremony was performed. Rogers had already accomplished a lot before the snows fell, but he wasn't satisfied. While other messengers traveled to nearby French forts, Rogers himself wanted to push on to Michilimackinac, the most isolated French fort.

Located near where Lakes Michigan, Huron, and Superior converged, Michilimackinac offered fur trading opportunities with all the tribes of the vast North American interior. Rogers had already heard stories about rich copper mines nearby and the possibility of a water route going all the way to the Pacific. Eager to claim this post for England, he set off from Detroit. But not even Rogers could traverse the ice floes of Lake Huron in December and he had to turn back, arriving in Detroit on December 21.

Not one to sit around over the holidays, Rogers left two days later for Fort Pitt with a small party of Rangers. They traveled by water to Sandusky Bay, and then overland from present-day Fremont along what was called the Great Trail. Rogers continued to rave about what he saw in Ohio, saying "the soil is not exceeded by any in this part of the world; the timber tall and fair; the rivers and lakes abound with a variety of fish, and here is the greatest plenty of wild water fowl of anywhere in the country. The woods abound with wild game. In a word, if peopled and improved to advantage, it would equal any of the British colonies on the sea coast."

After reaching Fort Pitt, Rogers left on his own and walked on to Philadelphia and then reached New York on February 14, 1761. He gave his report to Amherst and then returned to New Hampshire to try to adjust to peacetime. It was a transition he was never able to make. He did try to start out right by marrying into a family that offered him every advantage. On June 30, 1761, Rogers married Reverend Browne's nineteen-year-old daughter, Elizabeth, in her father's church. From his letters, Rogers appears to have been devoted to his Betsey, but in their seventeen-year marriage the couple rarely lived together.

Their regular separations were partly due to Rogers' efforts to get out of debt. Though his lifestyle did little to alleviate his condition, Rogers was also a victim of circumstances. He had already accumulated considerable debt by the time of his marriage due to his military affairs. At the time, officers who recruited troops stood personally liable for expenses until they could get approved payment from governmental authority. Rogers fell through the cracks of the system, as he was at various times representing the colonies of New Hampshire and Massachusetts, and was also classified as a regular British officer and a volunteer. His shifting status made it easier for colonial and federal governments to pass the buck and deny accountability. Rogers also did not help his cause by exaggerating his expenses and keeping slipshod records. When Rogers took on the royal accountants he was no more a match for them than the bean counters would be in attacking Rogers with a tomahawk.

Though he was allowed a portion of his claims, Rogers needed regular income to continue to stave off his creditors. He turned to General Amherst, who offered Rogers a captain's commission and a chance to go to South Carolina where the British army was putting down a Cherokee rebellion. Leaving his bride behind, Rogers headed south in 1761. He arrived too late for any fighting, but while in the Carolinas, he met people who told him more about the riches of the northwest, and a river that went through a place called Ouragon and all the way to the Pacific. He kept these thoughts for future reference.

Rogers found the peace time army unfulfilling and returned north in 1763. Here he was saved by the outbreak of Pontiac's Conspiracy. In the spring of 1763, the Ottawa chief

Pontiac had united the midwestern tribes who were upset that their French allies had given up and left them at the mercy of the haughty British for their trade goods. With a series of well-coordinated and organized attacks on the scattered Great Lakes forts, the Indians had destroyed every fort north and west of Fort Pitt except for one. The exception was Detroit, which was besieged and would have fallen except it was reachable by British warships.

A relief expedition was being organized under Captain James Dalyell, and Rogers was asked to join them. The troops sailed from Fort Niagara on July 10 and five days later arrived at the smoldering remains of Fort Presqu' Isle. This grim scene was repeated at Fort Sandusky on Sandusky Bay, and here Dalyell sent Rogers to destroy the nearest Indian village in retaliation. The expedition arrived at Detroit on July 29, and ran the gauntlet of the Detroit River to the joy of the besieged garrison.

Dalyell had a low regard for Indians as fighters and was convinced that British troops could fight their way out of the fort. On July 31, Rogers found himself once again sneaking out of a fort in the middle of the night into hostile territory as a part of a 247-man force. They got a few miles outside the gates before they were ambushed by a withering fire at a bridge that came to be called Bloody Bridge. Dalyell was killed, and 61 other men were killed or wounded as the British were forced back. Rogers covered the retreat, as he led a small group in an abandoned house who held off the Indians until the others could return to the fort. He continued fighting the rest of the night until a boat could be sent out at dawn to cover their escape with cannon fire.

Had Rogers been killed at Bloody Bridge he would have been remembered as a great American hero. However, his life was only half over, although he would never again fight in battle. The rest of his battles would be with his creditors, the authorities, and the bottle.

Rogers remained trapped in Detroit until the siege was finally lifted on October 31. Pontiac finally had to acknowledge that the French were not coming back and British warships could patrol the Great Lakes with impunity. No other Indian was ever able to organize as effective a coalition to threaten the whites.

Returning to civilian life, Rogers was besieged this time by creditors and briefly jailed for debt in New York. With no hope of relief here, Rogers decided to go to London to lobby for adjustment of his debts and to seek a position for himself. Sailing in March of 1765, he left Betsey behind but was accompanied by Nathaniel Potter, whom he had hired as his personal secretary to help him with record keeping and promotion.

Rogers was a great hit in London. His fame had preceded him across the Atlantic and everyone wanted to meet "the famous Major Rogers." His activities were regularly reported on in the *London Gentlemen's Magazine* and he entertained lavishly. Trying to impress the London elite did mean incurring more debts and the social whirl involved a lot of drinking, which was starting to become a problem for Rogers.

Yet he also found time to launch a literary career, as he is credited with writing three books during his year in London. His first self-published effort was *The Journals of Major Robert Rogers*, which covered the war period from 1755-1761. This was followed almost immediately by *A Concise Account of North America*, a travelogue that heralded America as a land of opportunity and endeavored to attract investors in both the country and the author.

William Johnson claimed that Rogers was virtually illiterate, but Rogers actually wrote quite well for someone who'd quit school when he was eight years old. The stark descriptions and immediacy to his *Journal* leaves little doubt that he wrote it himself. But the difference in style and more expansive nature of his second book made it likely that he had ghost writing help, probably from Potter, who was a graduate of Princeton.

Another interesting difference between the two books is their treatment of Pontiac. In his *Concise Account* he goes into great detail about how Pontiac stopped his party along Lake Erie and demanded to know why an English war party trespassed on his lands. In his original *Journal*, Rogers mentions being stopped by Ottawa braves but made no mention of the chief. It's possible that the chief who hailed Rogers in Ohio in November of 1761 was Pontiac and Rogers chose not to mention the then-unknown chief by name in his journal. It's more likely that Rogers decided that since it might have been Pontiac who stopped him, it would help book sales to say that it was, since by 1765 Pontiac was one of the few North Americans more famous in London than Rogers himself.

The idea of accentuating the drama of Pontiac reached its climax in the next work credited to Rogers. It was a play called *Ponteach: Or the Savages of America, A Tragedy*, where the noble savages are betrayed by the corrupt English. Although Rogers was surprisingly sympathetic to the Indians he fought, he almost certainly had no larger role than consultant for this work. A five act drama written in blank verse was well beyond his talents and might have been too much for Potter as well. Rogers never claimed authorship, but was still presumed to have written it. And as the only other American known to have written a play had recently died, Rogers was briefly considered America's greatest living playwright. Unlike his books, however, the play was savaged by critics and it was never produced.

Rogers had limited success in getting his accounts adjusted, although he did well enough to partially appease his creditors. But his lobbying efforts culminated on October 17, 1765 when he was presented to His Majesty, King George III. Not long afterwards, he was given an appointment as Commander and Superintendent of Fort Michilimackinac. This was the opportunity he had dreamed of. As the military commander and civil authority in charge of Indian and fur trade he could pursue the fabulously lucrative potential of the Northwest Passage.

Rogers failed to grasp that his getting the appointment had outraged both of his new bosses. Thomas Gage had replaced Amherst as military commander in North America and he had never liked Rogers. Indian Superintendant William Johnson liked to keep a tight rein on all fur and Indian trade and distrusted an independent operator like Rogers. Upon hearing of the appointment, Gage wrote to Johnson concerning Rogers: "he is wild, vain, of little understanding, and of as little principle... send me your advice in what manner he may best be tied up by instructions and prevented doing mischief and imposing upon you."

The new governor planned to take his wife along this time, and on June 3, 1766, Rogers and Betsey, as well as Potter, stopped at Johnson's house for final instructions. He was Sir William Johnson now, having been knighted after his victory at Lake George. And he lived at Johnson Hall, a suitably baronial mansion along the Mohawk River that everyone headed west to the Great Lakes had to pass by. Johnson gave Rogers strict instructions and exhortations to be frugal before sending him on.

Rogers arrived at Detroit, the outpost nearest Michilimackinac, early in August. It still took another full week of sailing to get to his new posting in the heart of the darkness of the American forest. The new commandant wasted little time in his pursuit of an inland empire. In September, he sent two of of his former Rangers, James Tute and Jonathan Carver, off to search for the fabled Northwest Passage. He gave these explorers the impression that their efforts would be sanctioned by the British government and they would be paid accordingly. Rogers' vision of a route to the Pacific was proved correct by Lewis and Clark forty years later, but he had seriously miscalculated the immense distance involved. In a year of traveling, Tute and Carver barely crossed the Mississippi before returning empty handed.

Rogers did prove to be popular with the Indians and fur traders whose conduct he was supposed to regulate. This was because he disobeyed his instructions regarding both. He was generous in giving presents to the Indians despite Johnson's urgings to be frugal with royal funds. And Rogers gave the traders a free hand, allowing them to spend the winter in Indian villages despite orders not to. Johnson wanted all fur commerce to pass by Johnson Hall, but Rogers allied himself with a faction of Montreal based traders who obviously favored the St. Lawrence River as a trade route. Rogers also entered into business partnerships with traders, a form of corruption that was widespread on the frontier, but was still illegal.

Johnson and Gage fumed at Rogers' apparent disobedience, but as his vouchers were in order, possibly due to Potter's help, they had little choice but to pay them. But their suspicions were further raised when they intercepted a letter to Rogers from an officer named Hopkins who had defected to the French. Illegally reading the letter, they read a plea from Hopkins encouraging Rogers to join him. After making a copy for Gage, Johnson forwarded the letter and decided to send a more trusted officer to handle Michilimackinac's fiscal affairs.

Captain Benjamin Roberts was sent as the fort's new commissary officer in the summer of 1767, and he and Rogers clashed constantly. Rogers chafed at new federal interference, and his drinking and combativeness increased. In addition, Tute and Carver returned in failure. Rogers' disappointment in their results was matched only by the explorers' chagrin in being told there were no funds to pay them. Growing more desperate, Rogers now devised a proposal where Michilimackinac should be made a separate royal colony with himself installed as governor. He wanted Potter to take this plan to his high-placed friends in London. But Potter refused and the garrison was shocked to see Rogers and Potter engaged in a fist fight.

Potter went to Roberts and told him that Rogers planned to turn the fort over to the French if his latest scheme was denied. Roberts sent Potter on to Montreal, where he wrote out a detailed affidavit accusing Rogers of treason. Potter then sailed for London, but died of illness at sea. But Gage now had enough evidence to order that Rogers be arrested. On December 6, 1767, Rogers was arrested by his second in command. And since Rogers had shown seven years earlier that travel to and from Michilimackinac was impossible in December, Rogers was forced to spend the winter in the guardhouse of his own fort.

Rogers and his wife were treated rudely in captivity as rumors swirled throughout the fort. Rogers was alleged to be planning to escape and plunder the fort's stores and join the French in New Orleans. It is a tribute to Rogers' near-legendary status that he was thought capable of hauling equipment to New Orleans at a time when travel to Detroit was impossible for anyone else.

Rogers was held until June, when he was shipped in irons to Detroit. Charged with treason, his trial was to be a military tribunal rather than a civil trial. But at least it was to be held in Montreal, where he remained popular. Because of difficulties in gathering witnesses, the trial was not held until October of 1768, and the now-pregnant Betsey returned to New Hampshire.

Although Rogers was on trial for his life, there was very little hard evidence against him. Potter's affidavit was the most damning, but with his death at sea it was not possible for Rogers to confront his accuser, a key component of English judicial doctrine. There was no evidence that Rogers had ever replied to the Hopkins letter, and it was no crime for him to open his mail, although it was for Johnson to open it first. And the various garrison gossip aired during the trial proved inconclusive and inconsistent. On October 31, Rogers was acquitted of all charges, although a vindictive Gage ordered that he remain jailed until the verdict was reviewed in London. Rogers therefore missed the birth of his only child, a son named Arthur, in February of 1769.

Though acquitted, Rogers was still removed from his position and now had a cloud as well as considerable debt hanging over his head. In order to clear his name and lobby for relief and funds he decided to go to London again. But after leaving his wife and child at home, he did not find similar success on this trip abroad.

His creditors wanted Rogers to succeed since that meant they were more likely to be paid. But if his prospects were dimmed the alternative was debtor's prison. The theory was that by holding the debtor hostage, his associates or loved ones might raise enough cash. But the reality was debtors languishing in jail for years with no way to earn money to get out. After three years of juggling and trying to hold off his creditors, Rogers became a victim of this system and was sent to London's notorious Fleet Prison in 1772. Ironically, his former adversary Roberts occupied a nearby cell.

Living in deplorable conditions, Rogers' health declined, and with alcohol available in jail, his drinking problems worsened. He tried various ways of gaining release, such as petitioning for payment of his Northwest Passage expenses, applying for a foreign service post in India, and even suing General Gage. What finally got him out of prison was reform of British bankruptcy laws in 1774. He was able to get a half pay pension as a retired army captain, but otherwise Rogers left England empty-handed.

He returned to America in August of 1775 in poor health and seeming older than his 43 years. The country had changed a great deal in his six-year absence, the most obvious difference being that America was now at war with England. Yet Rogers was so preoccupied with his fiscal affairs that he failed to notice the significance and extent of these changes.

As his sole source of income came from the British army, Rogers came under immediate suspicion and was arrested on October 22. He was released after promising not to take up arms against America. Rogers personally told George Washington of his love for his native land, but a suspicious Washington wrote that "Rogers being much suspected of unfriendly views against the country, his conduct should be attended to with some degree of vigilance and circumspection."

Rogers continued to meet with royal officials long after it was considered disloyal to do so, and he was again arrested and sent to Philadelphia. When he arrived there on July 1, 1776, John Hancock wrote immediately to Washington that "Major Rogers is under guard at the barracks, Congress having, by a particular appointment, had under consideration a momentous matter this day, which prevented their attending to him. My next [letter] will inform you, I hope, of some very decisive measures." The "momentous matter" that Hancock mysteriously alluded to was the Declaration of Independence, which Congress ratified while Rogers was in jail just a few blocks away.

Rogers was sent back to New Hampshire but escaped and offered his services to the British, who eagerly accepted. He was promoted to Lieutenant Colonel and assigned to recruit a regiment of rangers. But neither Rogers nor his new recruits could approach his previous success. Though he apparently fought with his usual courage in defending against an American raid in October of 1776, Rogers saw no other combat in the American Revolution.

He did apparently play a role in another sidebar in American history. Recent evidence has indicated that it was Rogers who discovered that Nathan Hale was an American spy. Apparently Hale, after entering New York City in September of 1776, chose an out-of-uniform Rogers to confide in, and Rogers turned him in, enabling Hale on the gallows to allegedly regret that he "had but one life to give" for his country.

The Americans by now reviled Rogers as a traitor. His wife sought a divorce at a time when divorce was so rare and scandalous that it could only be granted by an act of the state legislature. But when Mrs. Rogers detailed her complaints it was granted without contest in New Hampshire in 1778. By that time the British had replaced Rogers as regimental commander and the only duty he was entrusted with was being sent on recruiting missions.

Apparently Rogers' drinking was by now so out of control that he couldn't even be trusted as a recruiter. His commander in Canada complained that "he at once disgraces the service and renders himself incapable of being depended upon." His brother James lamented, "I am sorry his good talents should so unguarded fall prey to intemperance." Rogers was also in and out of jail until he sailed to London in 1782, never to see his native land again.

Rogers' final years were spent in a downward spiral. When he died in a London flophouse on May 18, 1795, one obituary commented that "a long confinement .... had reduced him to the most miserable state of wretchedness."

However, it was more than prison or alcoholism that led to the collapse of Rogers' fortunes. As a leader and a warrior, Rogers was charismatic and courageous. An intelligent man also, he was visionary enough to be among the first to see the enormous potential of the northwest. But in trying to grab too much of that bounty for himself, his overreaching contributed to his ultimate downfall.

CHAPTER TWO

John Connolly
"A man of intrigue and artful address"

John Connolly was a dangerous man. A loquacious liar with nefarious designs, he was a master of deception. He was a doctor who never saw a patient and an officer who never led troops in battle. But he nonetheless was a real threat to his native colony and country, both of which he betrayed with extravagant designs that, if successful, could have changed our history.

Connolly was born at Wright's Ferry in York County, Pennsylvania. He was the only child of John and Susanna Connolly, but this was the third marriage for his mother. She'd had five children by her first husband, who died in 1735, and four more by her second husband before his death in 1741. She then married John Connolly, an Irishman who had been a British officer. Some accounts mention John as being born around 1750 but it was probably earlier than that.

Susanna Connolly died in 1753, which may explain why her son followed the Catholic faith of his father rather than his mother's Presbyterianism. She did leave an estate sufficient for John to be sent to Philadelphia to study medicine. He never completed his studies or practiced medicine, yet he was referred to as Dr. Connolly all his life. Connolly had a taste for adventure, and he joined the British army in 1762 while still quite young. After serving in a campaign on the Caribbean island of Martinique, he returned to serve against the Indians in Pontiac's Conspiracy. Stationed on the frontier, he found he liked the west and decided to stay. Another factor in this decision was that his uncle was George Croghan, the noted fur trader and Indian agent operating out of Pittsburgh. Connolly probably worked for his uncle's business, as it was known he traveled extensively into Indian territory during this period.

In 1770, Connolly was living in Pittsburgh with his wife Susanna when he met George Washington for the first time. Washington was traveling west with his partner William Crawford to scout for bounty lands to pay fellow veterans of the French and Indian War. In the fall of the year they went down the Ohio as far as present-day Gallipolis, and seven of their known campsites were on the Ohio side of the river. They returned to Pittsburgh on November 21 and stayed briefly in the infant settlement before returning home. During this time they visited Croghan's home at Croghan Hall, four miles above town on the eastern side of the Allegheny, but they stayed at Sample's Tavern. Washington wrote, "We lodged at what is called the town," which he described as about twenty buildings located just outside Fort Pitt.

On their last night in town they "invited the officers and some other gentlemen to dine," and Connolly was among the guests. He made a good impression, as the normally reticent Washington called him "a very sensible intelligent man who had traveled over a good deal of this western country." Washington wrote in his diary that "Dr. Connolly is so much delighted with the lands and climate on this river that he seems to wish for nothing more than to induce one hundred families to go there to live that he might be among them. A new and most desirable government might be established here to be bounded, by his account, by the Ohio northward and westward." Connolly was a visionary who clearly saw the vast potential of the west and he was also intelligent, ambitious and energetic. But his form of "new government" turned out to be different than Washington's.

New government was just beginning to become an issue in the area, as British troops abandoned Fort Pitt as no longer needed in 1771. This meant there was no federal governmental presence in an area previously felt to be crucial. The importance of the Forks of the Ohio was first seen by Washington when he was a young Virginia militia officer. In 1753 when delivering warning letters to the French, who were building forts nearby, Washington had noticed the location and recommend that the Virginians build a fort there.

However, the French drove the Virginians off and built Fort Duquense on the site and then defeated and captured Washington and his men when they entered the area the next year. But in becoming the first American to bring wagons and artillery across the mountains, Washington had built a road from Cumberland, Maryland that Virginians would use to head west to the Ohio. His route would eventually become the start of the National Road. In 1755, Washington accompanied a British army under General Braddock along this route, but they were ambushed and routed within a few miles of their goal. The British were not able to capture the French fort, which they renamed Fort Pitt, until 1758 when General Forbes built a different road through the middle of Pennsylvania. Thus there were two routes to the Forks of the Ohio, which brought settlers from two different colonies. A steady stream of frontiersmen followed and established settlements as far west as Wheeling.

In this first frontier, it was uncertain even what colony was being settled. The Pennsylvania southern border with Maryland had been settled by British surveyors Mason and Dixon in 1768, but many colonies had no defined western boundary in their original charter, although Maryland did. As settlers gravitated west the various colonies simply created new counties. But when both Pennsylvania and Virginia claimed Pittsburgh, a conflict arose and Connolly seized the opportunity for power.

Pennsylvania, which was a proprietary colony administered by the Penn family, acted first in 1773, incorporating Westmoreland County with the seat of government at Hannahstown, near present day Greensburg. Virginia was a royal colony whose governor was appointed by the king. In 1772, he promoted John Murray, Earl of Dunmore, from governor of New York to the larger colony of Virginia. When the new governor went to Fort Pitt the next year, Connolly used his charm to make a first impression as good as he had with Washington. When Dunmore sought to press Virginia's claim to the Forks of the Ohio, he turned to Connolly. After forming the new District of West Augusta, Dunmore named Connolly "Captain Commandant of the militia of Pittsburgh and its dependencies."

On January 1, 1774 Connolly posted a printed notice to that effect in Pittsburgh and called for the militia to assemble before the end of the month and help set up a new government. For this, he was arrested by Pennsylvania magistrate Arthur St. Clair. He was released on his own recognizance after promising to return for trial in April. In the interim, Connolly appears to have decided to change from setting up a Virginia government to disrupting the Pennsylvania administration.

He showed up as promised at the Hannahstown Court House—but at the head of 150 armed men. They surrounded the court house and blocked all the entrances, and Connolly announced that the "magistrates had no right to hold court." The next day he took three justices of the peace to Staunton, Virginia under guard. They were later released, but Connolly's reign of terror was just beginning.

Given a free hand by Dunmore, Connolly handed out officers' commissions to henchmen who recruited an army of border ruffians. A group of Pennsylvania citizens led by William Crawford complained that "Mr. Connolly is constantly surrounded by a body of armed men. He boasts the countenance of the Governor of Virginia and forcibly obstructs the execution of legal process" and added that his "militia is composed of men without character and without fortune and who would be equally averse to the regular administration of justice under the colony of Virginia as they are under the province of Pennsylvania." Arthur St. Clair accused Connolly of recruiting his militia with a cask of rum, adding wryly that this was "a very effectual way of recruiting."

So rough was Connolly's band of desperadoes that Simon Girty was actually a moderating force. Girty was given a lieutenant's commission by Connolly and when one of his men attempted to strike a Pennsylvania wife with a rifle butt, Girty shoved it away.

With the Pennsylvanians focusing on civil government and not armies, the Virginians were virtually unopposed. They reoccupied Fort Pitt, which Connolly renamed Fort Dunmore. The militia roamed freely, killing livestock, searching and plundering homes and destroying outbuildings. They "appropriated" gunpowder from one man and beat him when he had the nerve to ask for a receipt.

Connolly himself was an enthusiastic participant in these depredations. He went to the store of a Pennsylvania fur trader, and in the absence of the owner ordered that the clerk be arrested. When the clerk asked permission to lock up the store first, Connolly refused, saying, "let the skins and the store go to the devil, if your master were here I would serve him in the same manner." He went to the home of a justice of the peace and, according to witnesses, "abused him in a blasphemous, outrageous manner, threatening to send him in irons to Virginia the next day."

The energetic Connolly rarely took a day off, for on Christmas Eve, he and Girty and some others went to the Westmoreland County jail and demanded custody of a prisoner held there. When the jailer hesitated, Connolly "threatened to tie and carry him off," and ordered that the jail roof be torn off. The jailer relented and Connolly personally snatched his prisoner.

In writing his account of this period, Connolly claimed "it was my endeavor, throughout to conduct myself with a dispassionate and candid regard to justice only." The Pennsylvanians who knew better began to flood officials with complaints about Connolly's conduct. A group of Pittsburgh citizens wrote to Governor John Penn that they "have suffered in an unprecedented manner by the arbitrary proceedings of Dr. Connolly since the commencement of his tyrannical behavior at Pittsburgh." A justice of the peace wrote "since the return of the celebrated Dr. Connolly from

Virginia…. Our village is become the scene of anarchy and confusion." A sheriff complained that "I am at a loss how to proceed in matters, as I am daily threatened of my life and property if I proceed to execute my office."

Governor Penn wrote to Lord Dunmore to protest Connolly's abuses, "I have so many complaints about the behavior of Dr. Connolly that I am obliged to wish your lordship to make some inquiry into the conduct which if my information be true, is extremely oppressive and tyrannical…. He seizes upon the property of the people without reserve and treats the persons of our magistrates with the utmost insolence and disrespect…. I would fain hope you would not encourage Mr. Connolly in such exorbitances as are laid to his charge." Dunmore not only supported Connolly but wrote to Penn and demanded that St. Clair be removed from office, a request that Penn considered "not only unreasonable but somewhat dictatorial."

Of all the charges Penn had listed against Connolly, the most serious was "there is great reason to fear his military operations may have a dangerous tendency to involve the colonies in a general Indian War." And Connolly did all he could to provoke hostile Indians into a war that he felt would strengthen Virginia's claims. It was always easy to start a war in the tinderbox that was the frontier, but it was especially easy in 1774.

Western settlement had slowed after Pontiac's Conspiracy when the king prohibited settlement west of the mountains. But at the Treaty of Fort Stanwix in 1768 the powerful Iroquois League, seeking to deflect expansion away from them, renounced their claims to Kentucky. They were not using this area, but it was a hunting grounds for the Shawnee. As settlers streamed west by either the Ohio River or overland through the Cumberland Gap, the Shawnee grew increasingly resentful.

Connolly sought to exploit this resentment by fanning the flames of war. By spreading rumors and issuing warnings it was easy to convince the populace that war was coming. In April of 1774, Connolly issued a circular in the Wheeling area that said war was inevitable and that everyone should be prepared. According to George Rogers Clark, the frontiersmen considered this to be a declaration of war that authorized pre-emptive strikes. A group of Virginians under Michael Cresap went out looking for Indians to scalp.

In one of those cases of frontier injustice that were all too common, the worst atrocity connected with Cresap was the one that he had no part of. Near present-day Steubenville was the village of the family of the Mingo chief Logan. He had long been friendly with the whites, and his family often crossed the river to trade at a white settlement called Baker's Bottom. On April 30, a group crossed over to get milk for the child of John Gibson, a fur trader who was married to Logan's sister. The whites got the Indians drunk, provoked an argument and then murdered thirteen members of Logan's family.

Although this outrage sent Logan on the warpath seeking revenge, the outnumbered Shawnee still hoped to avoid war. When a group of Pennsylvania fur traders led by Richard Butler sought to return home, Shawnee war chief Cornstalk sent a group of warriors under his brother to escort them through Indian territory. After arriving safely at Pittsburgh, Butler requested that Connolly arrange for the safe return of the Shawnee, but said Connolly "declared in a very ill natured manner he would not speak to them." Connolly then dispatched 40 militiamen to arrest the

Shawnee, who were safely hidden at Croghan Hall. After hearing that they had left on their own, Connolly then sent a party after them with orders to fire on them if they could catch them.

Connolly openly told St. Clair that his attitude towards the Shawnee was "I shall pursue every measure to offend them." Yet in writing his account of this era later, Connolly again stated the opposite of what his actions indicated, claiming that "every endeavor at pacification was employed by me, but unhappily without effect."

Lord Dunmore called out the Virginia militia in June, which guaranteed there would be war. The ensuing conflict was known as Lord Dunmore's War, but it could have just as easily been called Connolly's War. Yet once the campaign began, Connolly stayed out of harm's way as long as possible, claiming that he was needed at Fort Dunmore.

The Virginia legislature did not authorize funds to pay the militia, so the mercenaries were offered land grants and whatever plunder they could steal from the Indians. Connolly took advantage of this to claim and have surveyed a 4,000 acre tract at the Falls of The Ohio that today is occupied by downtown Louisville, Kentucky.

Dunmore ordered one group of militia under Andrew Lewis to come from the south up the Kanawha River to the Ohio. Dunmore planned to meet this force there but first he passed through the state recruiting. While he was still in the east, Connolly remained in charge at Pittsburgh. He sent troops out under William Crawford to build Fort Fincastle at Wheeling and Fort Gower at the mouth of the Hocking at present-day Hockingport.

Connolly also authorized a raid under Angus McDonald to the nearest Shawnee towns on the Muskingum near present-day Dresden. Among the officers on this raid were Daniel Morgan and George Rogers Clark. The future Revolutionary War heroes of Saratoga and Vincennes got their first taste of military command on this raid into Ohio. Dunmore arrived later in the summer at Pittsburgh and led his army down the Ohio.

The Shawnee needed to keep Lewis and Dunmore from meeting, and they attacked Lewis at Point Pleasant, West Virginia at the mouth of the Kanawha on October 10. After a fierce, all-day battle, the Shawnee had to retreat and both Virginia armies crossed into Ohio. At Camp Charlotte in Pickaway County they forced the Indians to accept harsh terms. Logan refused to attend the treaty conference and when pressed, gave an eloquent statement of grief that was translated by his brother-in-law John Gibson. After Logan's Lament, the Virginians returned to Fort Gower in November.

Lord Dunmore's War was a curious conflict. Named for the only combatant who was not an American, the war basically pitted a single colony against one tribe. Yet Dunmore's War had significance far beyond its narrow intentions. Americans had never defeated an Indian army without British troops and they now resolved they could "march and shoot with any in the known world." And as they were anxious to hear news from Continental Congress in Philadelphia or of trouble with the British in Boston, there was much discussion at Fort Gower. Under the leadership of Adam Stephen, yet another Dunmore veteran who became a general in the Revolution, the officers voted to ratify the Fort Gower Resolves, which warned the king that "as the love of liberty.... Outweigh every other consideration, we resolve that we will exert every power within us for the defense of American liberty." This Ohio-based declaration of independence came five months before Lexington and Concord and signaled a shift that would impact Connolly's plans. A spirit of colonial cooperation prevailed and the following year Benjamin Franklin of Pennsylvania and Thomas Jefferson and Patrick Henry of Virginia urged all parties to set aside their differences concerning the Pittsburgh area and work together against the British. This was done and in 1780 the western issue was settled peacefully, with Pittsburgh becoming a part of Pennsylvania and Wheeling going to Virginia.

After the campaign, Dunmore left Connolly in command of a 75-man garrison at Fort Dunmore. But in March of 1775 the legislature refused to fund the western posts and the forts at Pittsburgh, Wheeling and Point Pleasant were abandoned. Dunmore now advised Connolly to focus his efforts on winning the western Indians to the British side in the war that was quickly becoming inevitable. At the treaty at Camp Charlotte it had been agreed that Dunmore would meet with the Indians the following summer at Pittsburgh to make more permanent arrangements. But it became apparent that there were bigger problems to deal with and Dunmore would not be present.

His eponymous war was the highlight of Dunmore's popularity with the Virginians. In fact, by the summer of 1775 he could no longer safely set foot on his own colony and had retreated to a ship in Yorktown harbor. As Washington concluded in a letter to Connolly, "matters are coming to a point." But Connolly owed all his authority to the royal governor and had no intention of joining the push for independence.

Connolly presided over the Pittsburgh treaty conference in place of Dunmore in June. Even patriots who suspected Connolly said he acted fairly, though he later claimed to have duped them. After the conference, he traveled to Virginia with some Indian chiefs, ostensibly to finalize treaty details. But Connolly's real purpose was to present a plan to Dunmore to keep the west in British hands during the Revolution.

Arriving at Yorktown in August, Connolly proposed raising a regiment of frontier loyalists that would meet with the British at Detroit. Along with British troops scattered throughout the Illinois country and the allied Indian tribes they would take Fort Pitt and then launch an unexpected assault on the colonies from the west. By marching into Virginia they could split the colonies in half and free Dunmore from his ship.

Dunmore was sufficiently impressed with this plan that he sent Connolly on to Boston to offer it to General Thomas Gage, the British commander. Before leaving, Connolly wrote a letter to John Gibson concerning the Indians. Gibson was so trusted by the Indians that they requested to trade with him and Dunmore felt he would be a valuable ally in aligning the Indians with the British.

With characteristic hindsight, Connolly later maintained "I had reason to suspect Lord Dunmore reposed too much confidence in the gentlemen," but that didn't stop him. In his letter Connolly mocked those who displayed "what is now ridiculously called patriotic spirit" and "whose ill-timed folly must draw upon them inevitable destruction." He concluded by cautioning Gibson to "shun the popular error.... Act as a good subject, and expect the rewards due to your services." However, Gibson had already decided otherwise and he turned Connolly's letter over to his fellow members of the West Augusta Committee of

Correspondence, thereby confirming the suspicion that Connolly was a Tory.

Connolly's plot was further compromised in Boston when his servant defected to the Americans and informed Washington that Gage was meeting with Connolly. But Gage saw the merit in Connolly's plan. He gave orders to the western infantry and artillery to report to Connolly and authorized funds for arms and gifts for the Indians. Yet in an ironic twist, immediate implementation of Connolly's betrayal was delayed by Benedict Arnold. In 1775 an American force led by Arnold invaded Canada and temporarily controlled the St. Lawrence River, the only water route to Detroit. This meant Connolly had to proceed overland through American territory, where he might be recognized.

Connolly returned to Virginia where on November 5 he received a Lieutenant Colonel's commission in the British Army. Soon afterwards he left in the company of two fellow Loyalists who were to be officers in his regiment. Open travel became more risky as they neared Pittsburgh, and on November 19, Connolly was recognized at Hagerstown, Maryland, by a former soldier. He and his companions were arrested that night, but his plans that he had hidden in his saddle were not found. A more loyal servant destroyed them and helped smuggle pen and paper so Connolly could write to Dunmore, Pittsburgh, and Detroit. He sent these out with a comrade who managed to escape but who was recaptured before he got to Pittsburgh.

Connolly was transferred to a jail in Philadelphia, and was paraded by captors he deemed "ignorant and stupidly turbulent." Considered a serious threat, he was imprisoned for nearly five years. At first he was visited regularly by his father-in-law, Sam Sample, the Pittsburgh tavern keeper and merchant. Later his wife Susanna moved to Philadelphia, leaving the couple's only child back in Pittsburgh. But in November 1776, she revealed her husband's escape plans, renounced him and returned to Pittsburgh. The only other family he had any contact with was Thomas Ewing, a half brother from his mother's second marriage who was a general in the American army. Connolly was allowed some visits with Ewing until abuses curtailed his privileges.

His most notable violation was a failed escape attempt in December 1777. He and two companions got to the roof of the jail and tried to climb down using a rope made of blankets tied together. But the rope broke on the first try and the potential escapee fell almost 50 feet, which nearly killed him.

Connolly's main activity during his incarceration seems to have been complaining about his treatment. When the British captured Philadelphia in 1777, Connolly was taken to the jail in York, Pennsylvania where quarters were more cramped. As he had hoped to be exchanged for an American POW of equal rank, he was particularly disturbed at this development. In a formal complaint to Continental Congress about his conditions he denounced being "subject to all the indignities and low insults of an illiberal gaoler and turnkey, and placed upon the same footing as horse thieves, deserters, negroes, and the lowest and most despicable of the human race." He also complained about excessive security and the lack of heat and blankets and the horrible effect this was having on his health.

A response had to be made, lest the British use this as an excuse to mistreat American prisoners. But an investigation by an American physician concluded that "his situation was directly opposite to his representation" and that Connolly's health complaints were "merely of an hypochondriac nature." As for excessive security, it was pointed out that Connolly had been caught trying to escape and tried to smuggle letters out, so all security was justified. And as for being exchanged for an American colonel, the American report noted that "at the time he was taken he was not in arms or at the head of any party, but was clandestinely making his way to Detroit in order to join, give intelligence to, and otherwise aid the garrison of that place." This meant that Connolly not only was not eligible for exchange, but that he was eligible to be hanged as a spy. This course of action was never seriously considered by the Americans, but Connolly apparently felt it was.

If Connolly now feared his captors, they also still feared him as a potentially dangerous threat. It was rumored that, if released, he would join Iroquois raiding parties that were terrifying frontier settlements. In fact, when an Indian raid destroyed Hannahstown in 1782, many believed that Connolly was behind it as a final act of revenge against the Pennsylvanians. Fears like this kept him behind bars for a longer time but Connolly was finally paroled in July of 1780. He reported to the British commander at New York and offered to lead raiding parties in the west but was not given an assignment until the following year.

In 1781, Connolly was ordered to join Cornwallis's Army in Virginia, where he was placed in command of the Virginia and North Carolina loyalists. But he found the southern climate did not agree with his delicate constitution and after complaining of "putrescent effluvia" he was granted a leave of absence. While recuperating at a house near Yorktown, he was recaptured on September 21, 1781.

While being taken to the rear, he had a chance encounter with Washington that he described this way: "I was now to see a man with whom I had formerly been upon a footing of intimacy, I may say of friendship. Politics might induce us to meet like enemies in the field, but should not have made us personally so. I had small time for reflection; we met him coming on horseback to view the camp. I can only say the friendly sentiments he once publicly professed for me no longer existed. He ordered me to be conducted to the Marquis de la Fayette's quarters."

Connolly remained a prisoner this time until March of 1782, when the war was virtually over. Upon his release, he sailed for London, where loyalists whose property had been confiscated by the Americans could apply for compensation. Connolly submitted a detailed account asking for over 6,500 pounds and included a brief autobiography accompanied by statements from Dunmore and Gage. But British officials also had a hard time believing Connolly, and he was awarded only a fraction of his claims, with 475 of the 793 pounds being for confiscation of his Louisville lands.

Connolly then went to Canada, where many loyalists relocated after the war. But he did not give up on his plans to have the west in British hands. The new United States needed western expansion, as the vast lands west of the mountains were about the only collateral the nation had to offer. But expanding and protecting the western border was a risky proposition. The British had refused to honor their agreement to give up Detroit and were encouraging and supplying Indian war parties from there. And the Spanish, who controlled the port of New Orleans where all western commerce flowed, were also eager to control and contain westward expansion. And most importantly, the land that the

Americans needed to sell to finance their government was occupied by Indian tribes that did not want to give it up.

The citizens of Kentucky were in a unique situation in 1788 as America considered its new Constitution. Kentucky was actually a part of Virginia at the time but was dissatisfied with the lack of protection against Indian raids that the eastern government offered. Many Kentuckians wanted to enter the union as a separate state but some advocated the creation of an independent nation. Many citizens spoke of alignment with England or Spain, and both European nations sought to exploit this in order to limit U.S. growth and strengthen their own claims on the west.

Now working out of Detroit, Connolly began another intrigue. He began a correspondence with Samuel Parsons, a territorial judge of the newly established Northwest Territory headquartered in Marietta, concerning the opening of the Mississippi to American shipping. The governor of the Northwest Territory was Connolly's old nemesis Arthur St. Clair, who began to monitor Connolly's activities and ordered American troops to put him under surveillance should he enter the country.

This is what Connolly did in the autumn of 1788, when he came via the Maumee and Great Miami Rivers and entered into Kentucky. His stated purpose was to discuss his Louisville land claims, but his real goal was to look for an alliance between Kentucky and England. He met with several prominent Kentucky leaders and offered supplies and British soldiers to help Kentucky take New Orleans from the Spanish. Even though his intentions were known, Connolly could still be disarmingly charming. One Kentuckian he met with wrote that he spoke "with so much seeming sincerity that had I not before been acquainted with his character as a man of intrigue and artful address, I should in all probability have given him my confidence."

But Connolly met his match when he dealt with James Wilkinson in Lexington on November 8. Wilkinson was a former Revolutionary War general who came west after the war and played a prominent role in early Kentucky politics. It was known by Wilkinson (and everyone) that Connolly was representing British interests. But it was not known by Connolly (or anyone) that Wilkinson was in the pay of the Spanish as Agent Number Thirteen. Wilkinson, whom historian Frederick Jackson Turner has called "the most consummate artist in treason that our nation has ever possessed" had traveled to New Orleans the previous year and offered to become a Spanish informant in exchange for gold and the right to ship his goods on the Mississippi.

So Connolly's secret offer of 10,000 men to attack the Spanish was passed on to them and Wilkinson also used this information to further his own agenda. As they parted, Wilkinson warned Connolly that he risked being assaulted due to his nationality as the Kentuckians resented British support of Indian raids on them. This was the kind of intimidation that Connolly himself might employ, but Wilkinson took it a step further. He actually hired someone to attack Connolly, making sure that it was specified that it was because he was British. After this, Connolly slunk back across the Ohio on November 20.

Kentucky did enter the union as a new state, and Connolly retired to Canada on a pension. He attempted a comeback in 1799 when he tried to become the Deputy Superintendent of Indian Affairs for Canada. He managed to get the backing of the Duke of York, but local officials convinced the government that there were more qualified candidates. Connolly's last years were spent living modestly in Montreal with his second wife, Margaret. He died there after a long illness on January 30, 1813. He is almost completely unknown today, but this cunning sycophant, liar and bully could well have been one of the most infamous of frontier characters.

CHAPTER THREE

Simon Girty

"The very picture of a villain"

Few people in American history are as hated as Simon Girty. In his own lifetime he was viewed as a drunken renegade traitor who delighted in torturing Americans, and this reputation has persisted to this day. A closer look at the man reveals a more complex character capable of both doubt and noble deeds. And while a look at his background may not excuse his actions, it does help explain them and makes his story a compelling one.

The circumstances of Girty's birth and youth were rough. In 1737 an Irish immigrant named Simon Girty married Mary Newton in Lancaster County, Pennsylvania. Girty was engaged in Indian trading along the Susquehanna River north of present-day Harrisburg. The couple had their first son in 1739 and produced another son every two years until 1745: Thomas was born in 1739, Simon in 1741, James in 1743, and George in 1745.

This frontier family lived in poverty and the children received no education at all; Simon Girty was illiterate all his life. The family moved farther west briefly, but as "squatters" who did not hold legal title to the land they occupied, authorities burned their cabin and forced them to return. What little money they had the father spent on whiskey, and alcoholism was a condition passed on to at least two of his sons.

In 1751, the elder Simon Girty was killed in a drunken brawl with an Indian. John Turner, Girty's trading partner, killed the Indian responsible, and in 1753, married the widow Girty. This union produced another son named John the next year.

The outbreak of the French and Indian War meant chaos on the Pennsylvania frontier, especially after Braddock's army was defeated near the Forks of the Ohio in 1755. Indian raids increased and in July 1756 the family was forced to take refuge within the local stockade. Indians surrounded the fort and the garrison was persuaded to surrender rather than be massacred. The fort was burned and all settlers carried off as captives towards Pittsburgh.

The fate of Indian captives was always capricious. As raiding parties expected to be followed, any captive who could not keep up might be summarily executed. Captives who made it to the Indian villages could be adopted to replace an Indian loved one and would then be treated as one of the village. But if the next of kin rejected the new adoptee, the captive would be publicly burned at the stake.

John Turner was singled out for this torture. With his horrified family forced to watch, he was slowly burned to death, with his captors trying to prolong his agony for as long as possible. In August 1756, teenaged Simon witnessed his first burning at the stake, with his stepfather as the victim. There would be more. Afterwards the rest of the family was split up. A rescue party a few weeks later recaptured the eldest brother Thomas, but the other Girty boys were all sent to different tribes. The fifteen-year-old Simon was sent to live with the Mingo, while thirteen-year-old James was sent to the Shawnee and eleven-year-old George to the Delaware, as were young John Turner and the boys' mother.

Adolescence is traumatic enough without a drastic change of culture, and the Girtys remained with their respective tribes for three of their crucial formative years. But all three boys were treated well by their new families and even after they were repatriated at Fort Pitt they maintained close ties with their respective tribes. After treaty talks had resulted in returning all captives to Fort Pitt, Simon remained in the area.

He did not farm or learn a trade, but was able to maintain regular work as an interpreter. The Mingo tribe was a branch of the Seneca, which in turn was a part of the powerful Iroquois League of tribes. Simon had mastered the Seneca language, which was a useful skill to have in a town on the edge of the frontier. His illiteracy did not matter as Indian tongues were verbal only and between government work and the fur trade a skilled translator was valued. He had regular work for the next fifteen years.

As the Pittsburgh area grew, there came to be some question about whether the area was in the colony of Pennsylvania or Virginia. Both claimed the region, as neither colony had clearly defined western boundaries. Though Pennsylvanian by birth, Girty sided with the Virginians in this controversy. In 1774, he accepted a lieutenant's commission in the Virginia militia. This was issued by John Connolly, the local agent of the governor of Virginia, whose plan was to recruit a rough-hewn band to intimidate the Pennsylvania authorities who had already established a local civil government.

The Virginia militia of "men without property or character" ran wild, disrupting official business and threatening residents. Girty was apparently one of the more restrained adherents, as on one occasion he deflected a rifle butt aimed at the head of a housewife. However, on Christmas Eve, he and Connolly were prominent leaders of a group that threatened to tear down the Westmoreland County jail if a prisoner was not handed over to them.

The Virginia faction also sought to advance their cause by provoking a general Indian war that would require them to rescue the frontier. In this conflict, Girty played a larger role. In June of 1774, Virginia's royal governor, Lord Dunmore, called out the militia to subdue tribes that had been stirred up by murders committed by Virginia settlers. Girty joined this expedition as an interpreter and scout, as did another man named Simon Kenton.

Dunmore planned to lead one force from Pittsburgh down the Ohio to meet another army under Andrew Lewis that was advancing north up the Kanawha River. Girty was entrusted to ferry messages between the two groups and he left dispatches in a hollow tree at the mouth of the Kanawha. This was dangerous work, as the Indians hoped to keep the two armies from uniting. On October 10, they attacked Lewis at Point Pleasant where the Kanawha meets the Ohio. After a fierce battle, the Indians had to retreat. Unable to prevent the Virginians from uniting, they were forced to accept harsh peace terms.

As the Virginians crossed the Ohio and headed for Shawnee towns, they sent word for chiefs to gather to discuss treaty negotiations. One who refused to attend was Logan, a Mingo whose entire family had been murdered at the beginning of hostilities. When approached, he gave a speech that has been called "Logan's Lament," an address so moving that it was used as an example of Indian eloquence by Thomas Jefferson, in his book *Notes on the State of Virginia:*

"I appeal to any white man to say that if ever he entered Logan's camp hungry and he gave him not meat; if he ever came cold and naked, and he clothed him not. During the course of the last long and bloody war, Logan remained idle in his cabin, an advocate for peace. Such was my love for the whites that my countrymen pointed as they passed, and said, 'Logan is the friend of the white man.' I had even thought to have lived with you, but for the injuries of one man. Colonel Cresap, the last spring, in cold blood and unprovoked, murdered all the relations of Logan, not even sparing my women and children. There runs not a drop of my blood in any living creature. This called on me for revenge. I have sought it; I have killed many; I have fully glutted my vengeance. For my country I rejoice at the beams of peace; but do not harbor a thought that mine is the joy of fear. Logan never felt fear. He will not turn on his heel to save his life. Who is there to mourn for Logan? Not one!"

There is some confusion as to whom this speech was delivered. It was definitely written down by John Gibson, a fur trader, who had been married to Logan's sister until she was murdered in the attack that so enraged Logan. But one eyewitness said it was Girty who approached Logan and memorized the speech for the literate Gibson to record. Gibson, whose reputation for honesty was so great that Indian tribes requested he be assigned to them, made a sworn statement several years later that the speech was first uttered to him. Both men were fluent in Logan's Seneca language, but as a relative Gibson would have been a logical choice to approach Logan. Nothing was said about this issue at the time, but in later years, Girty's antipathy towards Gibson was among the strongest of his many hatreds.

After the conclusion of Lord Dunmore's War, it became apparent that the impending conflict between America and England would become more significant than the quarrel between Pennsylvania and Virginia. Connolly remained loyal to England and made a list of people he felt were also loyal to the King, and Girty was on this list. Gibson was on this list as well, but when Connolly tried to recruit him, Gibson turned his letter over to the American forces that he sided with and Connolly was arrested.

Girty aligned himself with the Americans, but he was always regarded with suspicion and was no doubt conflicted. However, he was entrusted with key jobs because of his linguistic abilities. In 1775, the Virginia legislature sent him as a translator with James Wood to key Indian towns in Ohio to invite representatives to attend a conference at Pittsburgh. On May 1, 1776, Girty was appointed interpreter for the Six Nations, but he was discharged three months later "for ill behavior" that was unspecified. It might have been for drunkenness, which was always a problem for Girty, or it may have been doubts of his loyalty. He was actually arrested once in 1777 on suspicion of disloyalty but nothing came out of it and charges were dropped.

Girty also enlisted in the Continental Army and recruited others in the hopes of getting an officers' commission. But he was only made a lieutenant instead of a captain and his enthusiasm waned. When his regiment was sent to South Carolina, Girty remained behind. He continued to work as an interpreter for the Americans. In December of 1777, John Gibson, who was now a colonel and second in command at Fort Pitt, wrote to George Washington that, "Simon Girty, a messenger dispatched by General Hand to the Seneca towns on the head of the Allegheny, returned here a few days ago." On this mission, Girty had been accused of being a spy by the Seneca and held against his will but had managed to escape.

General Edward Hand was in charge of the Western Department headquarters at Fort Pitt, though he had no regular army troops under him. Forced to work with local militia, he felt pressured to make some accomplishments. When he heard of a cache of British supplies supposedly hidden along the Cuyahoga River, he decided to go after it in February of 1778. Girty went along as interpreter. Hand's force found no supplies and few Indians to attack, but they did encounter plenty of miserable weather. The only Indians seen were a handful of squaws and children, who were all killed. They turned out to be relatives of Captain Pipe, a chief of the Delaware tribe that the Americans were trying to keep from aligning with the British.

Girty's only known role in this campaign was when he was asked to judge which Americans could claim to have murdered a particular Indian boy, which was hardly the glory he had anticipated. The dispirited Americans never got to the Cuyahoga and returned ingloriously. Their winter adventure was derisively referred to as the Squaw Campaign.

By now Girty was as disillusioned with the American cause as he was with his hopes to advance in it. He was ripe for temptation that appeared in the form of Matthew Elliott. A fur trader who had been taken to Detroit, Elliott was convinced the British headquartered there were in a better position to win. After returning to Pittsburgh by way of Canada, he began to recruit for the British.

His primary target was Alexander McKee, the Indian agent who had succeeded George Croghan. As the only royal employee on the frontier, McKee was suspected of British sympathies, but he was needed because his knowledge of Indian affairs might keep the tribes neutral. He professed loyalty to the Americans, but suspicion of him increased so much that he was placed under house arrest. He was ordered to go east to face trial but convinced Hand that he was currently too ill to travel.

On March 28, 1778, a vast reservoir of Indian knowledge left Pittsburgh for Detroit. Hand had to report, "I have the mortification to inform you that Alexander McKee made his escape from this place, as also Matthew Elliott, a person lately from Quebec on parole, Simon Girty, Robert Surplus and one Higgins." This defection threw the frontier into an uproar, with McKee felt to be the major loss.

En route to their new headquarters at Detroit, the deserters stopped at Indian towns to announce their intentions. At the Delaware towns on the Tuscarawas they spread rumors that the Americans were defeated and heading west to kill Indians. The alarmed Delaware considered joining the British until Moravian missionaries living among them were able to prove the rumors to be false. In Shawnee country, the defectors added to their ranks James Girty, who had been living with that tribe as a trader.

Arriving at Detroit in June, this crew was welcomed by British commander Henry Hamilton. Girty was put on the payroll as an interpreter sind instructed to live among the Mingo. Though he fought alongside the tribe, he was never in command of Indian forces, as many have believed. In fact,

Girty never attained higher rank than the lieutenant's commission he held as a marauder for Connolly, as the British gave him no military rank at all.

Since he had held rank in the American army, Girty was considered a deserter and was charged with treason in June of 1778. Later, a bounty of $800 was offered for him as American hatred of him increased. But Girty apparently had some initial doubts about his desertion, as he expressed them to an old friend he encountered that fall in the course of a raid to Kentucky.

Simon Kenton had crossed the Ohio River from Kentucky to steal Indian horses and had been captured. He was treated roughly, being forced to run the gauntlet at several villages and had been painted black, which meant he was marked for burning at the stake. In this condition he was interrogated by Girty at Wapatomica, at the present site of Zanesfield. When Girty found that the prisoner was his old friend, his brusque manner changed.

He embraced his friend, promised to help him, and expressed remorse that he had been "too hasty" in abandoning the American cause. True to his word, Girty went to great lengths on Kenton's behalf. He made impassioned pleas for his life and was able to forestall execution long enough that custody could be transferred to the British at Detroit. But Girty's regrets about deserting ceased once he found out how the Americans felt about him.

By November of 1778, Hand had been replaced at Fort Pitt by General Lachlan MacIntosh, who also arrived with Continental soldiers. MacIntosh planned an assault on Detroit, but his army started late and moved slowly through the Ohio wilderness. With winter approaching, the Americans decided to build a fort to use to launch an invasion the next year. They built Fort Laurens on the Tuscarawas at present-day Bolivar, which could also be used to protect the nearby Moravian mission towns along the Delaware. The commander of the 180-man garrison was John Gibson.

In January of 1779, Girty and a party of seventeen Mingo braves were sent to reconnoiter the situation. They stopped at the Moravian mission towns, as many war parties did. The Moravians were supposed to be neutral, but they actually provided the Americans with valuable information while being forced to offer hospitality to Indian war parties. Missionary David Zeisberger now wrote to Gibson that Girty was in the area, and had professed a personal desire to take Gibson's scalp.

Gibson did not feel too threatened, as he wrote to MacIntosh saying, " I hope if Mr. Girty comes to pay a visit, I shall be able to trepan him." But MacIntosh was never able to read of Gibson's plans to drain the brain of Girty, because on January 22, the party carrying this and other letters was attacked by Girty's Mingoes three miles from the fort. The troops fought their way back to the fort but the courier was captured with valuable dispatches that revealed the weakness of the Americans' position.

Girty had to take these letters back to the Sandusky area to have them read, but he was enraged to hear what Gibson had said about him. Knowing now that he could never return to the American side, he resolved his doubts with a hostility towards his former allies that never wavered again. After the message bearer had been burned at the stake, Girty lobbied British and Indians alike for a larger force to attack Fort Laurens.

Command of this expedition fell to Captain Henry Bird, an engineer from the 8th Regiment. Bird had been appalled by the burning of defenseless American captives and had upbraided the Indians for their conduct, but he still went along on the raiding party. On February 25, about 200 British and Indians surprised a wood-cutting detail outside the fort, and killed and scalped all seventeen members within sight of the garrison. They besieged the fort for the next 25 days, reducing the garrison to boiling and eating their own moccasins for sustenance. However, the impatient Indians were also hungry and they abandoned their siege in March.

Girty correctly suspected that the Moravian missionaries had warned Gibson about him and made a personal effort to take them out of the picture. While near Coshocton on a mission to retrieve some letters left in a hollow tree, he encountered Zeisberger. He is alleged to have tried to kill him but was prevented by the sudden arrival of witnesses. Girty continued to threaten and intimidate the Moravians whenever possible. The antipathy was mutual, as missionary John Heckewelder called Girty "as brutal, depraved, and wicked a wretch as ever lived."

George, the youngest Girty, joined his brothers at Detroit in August of 1779. He had previously been an officer in the U.S. Navy on an unusual mission. In January 1778 an armed galley cheerfully named the *Rattletrap* had left Pittsburgh bound for Natchez. Commissioned by the navy, the ship's mission was to seize property from British loyalists living on the lower Mississippi and then proceed to New Orleans. Here they would sell their goods and use the funds to purchase much needed gunpowder and supplies from the Spanish authorities there. They were basically river pirates, but George Girty soon deserted and joined the British at Detroit.

The Spanish who controlled New Orleans were officially neutral but were eager to hinder the British, who they considered their main rivals for control of the American west. They secretly sold supplies to the Americans, and one such party under David Rogers came up the Mississippi and Ohio in September 1779. At the future site of Cincinnati, their five-boat flotilla was attacked by a band that included Simon and George Girty. Only one boat got away and George Rogers Clark lamented "the capture of Colonel Rogers' boats is a very great loss." On the British side, Girty's stature rose with this success.

Soon afterwards, the Spanish joined the French in the war against England, which led to some unique developments in the Revolution in the west in 1780. For example, that spring the Kentuckians under Clark built Fort Jefferson on the Mississippi. Since Kentucky was a county of Virginia, this meant that Virginia was maintaining a fort on the Mississippi River. Stranger yet was when the Spanish from St. Louis attacked the British post at St. Joseph near Lake Michigan—surely the only time the Spanish army ever invaded Michigan. And later that summer, a French cavalry officer came to Fort Pitt on a secret mission. Accompanied by the sister of Chief Cornstalk, a six-foot tall Shawnee woman known as Grenadier Squaw, he traveled to Vincennes to lead French fur traders there on an unsuccessful assault on Detroit. And in a final oddity, the British carted artillery through the roadless length of Ohio into Kentucky, and in this endeavor, Girty played a major role.

Indian raiding parties had been harassing the Kentucky settlements for several years, but usually after the initial surprise, the Kentuckians holed up safely in their stockades until the raiders left. But the stockade walls were no match for artillery, so Captain Bird and a 700-man force that included all three Girtys came south with two cannons in June of 1780. Their original goal was Louisville and some larger forts, but the Indians insisted on attacking some smaller forts first and Bird acquiesced.

They first surprised Ruddle's Station on Kentucky's Licking River. After firing two cannon shots, the British sent Girty to the fort under a flag of truce to demand surrender. The garrison realized the fort's walls would not hold and they risked being massacred, so the surrender had nothing to do with Girty or his presentation. But after opening the gates, several settlers were killed by Indians before Bird could bring them under control. The Indians then took their hostilities out on livestock and butchered all the fort's cattle.

Slowed down by their captives, Bird's force next went to nearby Martin's Station, which also surrendered. By now the British had several hundred captives to feed, but the Indians had killed off the livestock that might have fed them. Instead of taking other forts, they were forced to return to Detroit in such haste that they left their artillery at James Girty's trading post at present day Fort Loramie.

Early in 1781, the British authorities assigned Girty to live among the Wyandot tribe. Though he lived almost exclusively among the Indians for five years, Girty was not quite the savage white renegade he was made out to be. Most of his life, he dressed and lived as a white man, and living with whatever tribe he was told was his job. He learned the Wyandot language, though he was not as fluent as he was in

Seneca, and he also accompanied his new tribe on raiding and war parties.

Though illiterate, Girty was intelligent enough to learn several Indian languages. And though he could be cruel, he also is known to have taken an active part in saving several captives from torture. He was particularly empathetic to young boys who were about the same age as he was when he was captured. And he was an able and loyal employee of the British government. Captain Bird, whose temperament could not have been any more different from Girty's, wrote to his commander, "Girty, I assure you, sir, is one of the most useful, disinterested friends in his department that the government has."

But to the Americans, Girty was the most hateful of traitors and was blamed for every raid. Not only did he lead terrorizing Indian war parties into an area he knew, but the victims were often his former neighbors. Girty couldn't have possibly been at all the places he was accused of, but as the most infamous of three brothers, he got blamed for the misdeeds of any of them. George again lived among the Delaware and was most notable for military exploits, while James among the Shawnee was more involved with trading and commercial ventures. James was also the only Girty brother who didn't drink to excess, but apparently he was as cruel when sober as his brothers were when drunk.

The only frontier leader as widely reviled as Simon Girty was Joseph Brant, the Iroquois war chief. Brant led a series of brutal raids against settlers in upstate New York and Pennsylvania to establish his reputation. In 1781, Brant was sent to Detroit to help, as by then there was almost nothing left to burn in his theater of war.

Brant was an interesting contrast to Girty. His sister had been the Indian mistress of the powerful Indian agent Sir William Johnson, and he therefore had a privileged upbringing. He was educated by the founder of Dartmouth College, became a Christian who translated the Bible to Mohawk, and had even joined the Masons. He had traveled to London where he socialized with royalty and was profiled by James Boswell and had his portrait painted by Gilbert Stuart. He was considered to be the most civilized of Indians, while Girty was considered the most savage of white men.

Yet the two had much in common. Both were fluent in English and Seneca and had their feet in both white and Indian worlds. Both were brave and fierce warriors who had associations with atrocities. And both had large egos and large appetites for alcohol. Brant later killed his oldest son in a drunken brawl, although apparently in self-defense.

In 1781 George Rogers Clark was planning to finally capture Detroit with the help of federal troops. He had already had much success as head of the Kentucky militia, but now he hoped to get John Gibson and his regiment to accompany him. However, the commander at Fort Pitt refused to release Gibson or his men, so Clark tried to get Pennsylvania militia to join him. A 100-man contingent under Colonel Archibald Lochry was hurrying downstream to catch up with Clark when they were ambushed near the mouth of the Miami River on August 24. The attack was led by Brant and George Girty, who succeeded in killing or capturing the entire party.

A few days later, the victors were joined by Simon Girty, and that night the two most hated men on the frontier got drunk together. As they boasted of their respective prowess, Girty called Brant a liar and Brant responded by slashing Girty's forehead with his saber. Girty nearly died and it took several months for him to recover. His wound left an ugly scar that he gave differing stories about later. It also may have contributed to his increasingly violent personality and possibly his eventual blindness.

The Revolutionary War in the west lagged about a year behind the east. Although the conflict started later, the year after the American victory at Yorktown was one of the bloodiest of the war, and Simon Girty was involved in most of the tragic events of 1782. His enemies, the Moravians, had been forcibly removed from their towns after warning Wheeling residents of an impending attack the previous fall. The Christian Indians, mainly Delaware, had been taken into harsh protective custody near Upper Sandusky, but the white missionaries were to be sent to Detroit under suspicion of treason.

Girty gleefully announced this news to the missionaries and ordered their escort to drive them like cattle all the way around Lake Erie to Detroit. Girty then left with a war party. But the Frenchman who was to escort the missionaries offered the sixty-year-old Zeisberger his own horse and took the Moravians only as far as Lower Sandusky (present-day Fremont), where they waited for a British ship to take them across the lake.

They were still waiting when Girty's party returned with scalps and captives. According to Heckewelder, when Girty saw his orders had been disobeyed he "behaved like a madman… he swore the most horrid oaths respecting us and continued in that way after midnight. His oaths were all to the purport that he would never leave the house until he had split our heads in two with his tomahawk and made our brains stick to the wall… he had somewhere procured liquor and would at every drink renew his oaths, which he repeated until he fell asleep."

Even a drunken Girty would have realized it would be unwise to murder the people he had been ordered to send to headquarters, so he may have just enjoyed terrorizing the missionaries. Though not a cold-blooded killer, Girty was a mean drunk, and he was frequently drunk. Fortunately for the Moravians, a boat appeared the next day and took them to Detroit, where they were treated well and released.

Their Christian converts did not fare as well. Over 90 of them had been permitted to return to their village at Gnadenhutten to retrieve unharvested corn. But raiding parties like Girty's had been active that spring and had used the abandoned town as a way station. Pennsylvania militia tracking the raiders found stolen items at the town and blamed the Moravians. On March 8, 1782, they murdered 96 men, women and children and burned their bodies and the town.

After murdering the Christian Indians who had previously helped warn them of the raids, the militia felt emboldened enough to launch an invasion of the Sandusky region. William Crawford, Washington's old friend, was narrowly elected commander of the 480-man expedition over David Williamson, who had supervised the Gnadenhutten Massacre. No federal troops could be spared for this expedition, although the commander did offer the services of his chief surgeon, Dr. John Knight.

This army lumbered through Ohio and was watched all the way. They were attacked by a combined British and Indian force on June 4 as they approached Upper Sandusky. After inconclusive fighting, the battle continued evenly the next day until British and Indian reinforcements arrived.

Girty fought alongside his Wyandots and there is an unsupported legend that he warned Crawford after the first night that he was about to be surrounded.

Now facing larger numbers, Crawford ordered a retreat, but became separated from most of his troops in the confusion. He and Dr. Knight and some others were captured while Williamson led the retreat back to Fort Pitt. With Indian rage over Gnadenhutten still high, Crawford knew he was in trouble, and he sought the help of Girty, who he had known since before Lord Dunmore's War. Girty was alleged to have said he would try to help but he had little leverage with the Delaware who had lost kin at Gnadenhutten.

The only account available of the next day is Knight's, and his story is the damning indictment of Girty that is most prevalent today. Knight reported that on June 10 he and Crawford were taken to a village on Tymochtee Creek and their faces were painted black. Crawford then asked Girty if he was to be burned and Girty confirmed that he was.

Crawford was then stripped and tethered to a pole and after an Indian speech, he was charged by Indians who shot about 70 loads of gunpowder all over his body at point blank range. As the fire burned, his ears were cut off and he was poked with burning sticks. After a while he had only hot coals to stand on or walk on, and in agony he begged Girty to shoot him. Girty at first ignored him, then replied that he had no gun and turned to a companion and laughed.

It has been pointed out in Girty's defense that there is non-mirthful laughter and that Indians sometimes ordered whites to laugh at victims being tortured. Some have said that he tried to help until threatened with taking Crawford's place. But there is no supporting evidence of this, although official British reports do mention that Matthew Elliott tried to halt the execution. In addition, Girty rode several miles to witness Crawford's execution rather than boycott it. Knight was the only literate survivor present and he presents a grim account. He says Girty calmly tried to engage him in conversation as their mutual friend was being tortured to death.

When Knight had offered his hand to Girty earlier, Girty had called him a "damned rascal" and ordered him off. But now he approached Knight, told him to expect the same, then asked what the Americans thought of him and would they hurt him if they caught him. He then went on to "express a great deal of ill will towards Colonel Gibson, saying he was one of his greatest enemies." The horrified doctor "paid little attention" to Girty's ramblings. After Crawford had been scalped but was still alive, the scalp was thrown in Knight's face before he was led off. Knight later escaped and gave the account most responsible for Girty's reputation.

After defeating the Pennsylvania forces, the British and Indians next turned their attention towards Kentucky. A large party that included Girty attacked Bryant's Station in August. After the initial surprise assault, the raiding party moved on and the reinforced settlers chased after them. This was normal procedure after a raid but the Kentuckians were surprised to see a small party of Indians leisurely camped along the Licking River on August 19.

Some men such as Daniel Boone suspected a trap, but an officer named Hugh McGary called for all men who weren't cowards to follow him. Their manhood having been questioned, the Kentuckians all followed McGary into a deadly ambush that resulted in over 70 deaths, including

Boone's teenage son. Girty was said to have been in charge at the Battle of Blue Licks, but was only fighting along with his Wyandot warriors.

The war in the east was already over and after the bloody 1782 campaigns the western war was also winding down. In Paris, the Americans and British were discussing peace terms that would result in a free and independent United States. In May of 1783, Girty was on a raid that brought him just a few miles from his former home at Pittsburgh. He was with a young captive when they heard a cannon shot from the fort. The captive explained that it was to celebrate the peace and independence that had been ratified. It was a bitter irony for Girty to be so near his home when he found out that he could never go there again. But unlike at Fort Laurens, he treated his messenger well and returned to Detroit.

Girty could no longer visit his relatives in Pittsburgh because he was so hated there, but they could visit him at Detroit. In the summer of 1783, his brother Thomas and stepbrother John Turner, who had remained loyal Americans, paid a visit. And with peace at hand the 42-year-old Girty now could start a family of his own. In 1784 he married Catherine Mallott, an attractive eighteen-year-old who had been taken captive along the Ohio River a few years earlier. The couple had four children, and of the two sons, one was named for Girty's older brother and the other for a friend in the British army, which shows that Girty was capable of forming loyal and lasting relationships with family and friends.

Girty still passionately hated the Americans, and he was still in a position to do something about it. After the Revolution, the Americans considered the Indians a conquered people and sought to take their lands to sell and settle. The British were reluctant to give up their lucrative Indian fur trade and wanted to keep the United States from expanding westward, so they continued to supply and encourage Indian raids. They also refused to give up their forts at Detroit and other Great Lakes locations.

As an interpreter who had the respect of the Indians, Girty always had plenty of work. Though now a family man who had a 160-acre farm on the Canadian side of the Detroit River, he was still sent by the British to various conferences. As the tribes sought to unify to check American expansion, Girty attended inter-tribal conferences at Niagara in 1786 and the Maumee Rapids near present-day Toledo in 1788. Though employed as a translator, he actively aligned himself with the pro-war faction.

In 1787 the United States organized the Great Lakes region into the Northwest Territory and settlement began across the Ohio River the next year. In response to sporadic raiding, American troops marched into Indian territory in 1790. Near present-day Fort Wayne, Indiana, U.S. soldiers were lured into an ambush by a tribal coalition. Encouraged by this victory, Indians stepped up their raids, and the next few years saw bloody border warfare that would determine whether the new nation could protect and expand its borders. It was during this period that Simon Girty reached the peak of his influence.

In January 1791, Girty was with a 300-man war party in the Cincinnati area. At Dunlap's Station, twelve miles up the Miami River, they surprised a surveying party and took a captive named Abner Hunt. The fort was defended by 35 men, including thirteen soldiers recently sent from Cincinnati. Girty forced Hunt to plead for the fort to surrender, and their refusal doomed the captive. Hunt was stripped and tied to the ground and slowly tortured to death with a fire kindled in his abdomen. The horrified garrison had to hear his cries of agony all night before they finally grew weaker and ceased. Girty had seen his share of torture since watching his stepfather die, and he had prevented some from suffering such fates. But he is the only man known to have been actively involved in the two most famous stake burnings in Ohio history.

The Indian coalition was not only successful in raids, but that fall they administered the worst defeat ever suffered by the U.S. Army. A 1,500-man army under Territorial Governor Arthur St. Clair left Cincinnati's Fort Washington and moved slowly north under the watchful eyes of Indian scouts. On November 4, 1791 an Indian army surprised the Americans at the present-day town of Fort Recovery. After a brief fight, the Americans broke ranks and ran off in panic, leaving behind not only artillery and provisions but many of their wounded.

Girty fought with his Wyandots in this battle, and was presented with three of the American cannon as a trophy, although with no way to transport them, the field pieces had to be dismantled and hidden. He also played a more gruesome role in the battle's aftermath going through the casualties and pointing out officers he knew whose scalps would be more valued. One of these was the mortally wounded General Richard Butler, St. Clair's second in command and an acquaintance of Girty's from his Pittsburgh days.

The Indian coalition now clearly had the upper hand. New settlement came to a standstill and raiding parties now focused their efforts on supply convoys traveling between

American forts. Girty was on one such raid at Fort Jefferson in June of 1792, and may have been involved in many others as well.

A boy named O.M. Spencer who was taken captive about this time provides a good description of Girty. Spencer was being held in the village of the Shawnee chief Blue Jacket, who, along with Little Turtle, was the major leader of the Indian coalition. Blue Jacket was expecting a visit from Girty and to show how highly Girty was thought of, he had dressed in all his best clothes, including a red coat with epaulets, a sash, silver gorget, and medallion.

Girty appeared in plain clothes, and Spencer thought he looked "the very picture of a villain." Girty stood about 5'9" and was stocky and muscular with black hair and deep piercing eyes. He wore a bandana instead of a hat and carried two pistols and a knife in his belt. He questioned Spencer at length and complained of the "wrongs he had received at the hands" of the Americans and boasted of the revenge he had taken. Then he raised his bandana to show his scar that he claimed was given to him by an American in St. Clair's army before Girty had sent him to hell. To support his bellicose image, Girty told another captive his goal was to "raise hell to prevent peace."

In October 1792 an Indian conference was held at the Grand Glaize, where the Auglaize and Maumee Rivers meet in present-day Defiance. Over 3,000 braves attended, which made it the largest Indian conference ever held up to that time. British authorities fed and supplied the Indians, but only one white man was permitted to attend the meetings. That man was Simon Girty. Some Indians, led by Joseph Brant, had advocated letting whites settle as far west as the Tuscarawas and Cuyahoga Rivers. But Girty's pro-war faction succeeded in diplomatically marginalizing Brant, insisting that no white settlers be allowed across the Ohio.

The Americans were in a poor bargaining position, but asked if their peace commissioners could meet with Indian leaders the next year. The Indians, with British help, would not let the Americans get any closer than the Detroit River, where they met a limited delegation that included Girty as a translator. Heckewelder, who was with the Americans, wrote that Girty "supported his insolence by a quill or long feather run through the under part of his nose crossways." More importantly, he was caught at least once mistranslating in order to make war a more likely outcome. Girty was never one to agonize over whether the ends justified the means. On another occasion he asked a fur trader to write a letter for him that made accusations against a rival. When the trader asked if the charges were true, Girty replied that it didn't matter if they were true or not.

Girty didn't usually have to resort to lies to intimidate. At Detroit an American was visiting in hopes of reclaiming a relative held captive. Girty entered the home he was visiting, without knocking and in a drunken state. He stared at the American at length without speaking until he was asked if he had seen the American before. He replied, "No, but if I ever see you again, I shall know you," and then threw his knife near the feet of the American.

In the spring of 1794, the British showed support for their Indian allies by building Fort Miamis on the Maumee Rapids. Girty was kept busy with supplies and arrangements as the Indians became convinced the British were going to fight the Americans alongside them. But having gotten the war they wanted, the Indians should have been warned to be careful what they wished for. The Americans were now led by General Anthony Wayne, who had spent two years intensively training an army that was vastly superior to St. Clair's.

In June a large Indian party that included Girty went south to disrupt American supply routes. They attacked Fort Recovery, which had been built at the site of St. Clair's Defeat, and found that Girty's trophy cannon had been found and were used against the attackers. After driving off the Indians, Wayne's army confidently advanced towards the heart of Indian country. As he passed the Grand Glaize and headed towards Fort Miamis, the Indians attacked at a stand of fallen timbers along the Maumee on August 20. With Girty as a spectator, since the British were supposed to be neutral, the Americans dealt the Indian coalition a fatal blow.

Girty continued to agitate for war, but the Indians had had enough. At the Treaty of Greene Ville the next year they gave up their rights to much of Ohio, beginning a 100-year process where they steadily lost land to the Americans. As a result of this, the British agreed to surrender Detroit and all other Great Lakes forts in 1796.

An outraged Girty vowed he would stay until American soldiers drove him out. Though a brave man, he had a real fear of what the Americans might do if they captured him. So when he saw the first boatload of soldiers approach Detroit, he allegedly jumped his horse off a steep bluff and swam across the Detroit River to Canada.

He remained on his farm there for most of the rest of his life. His drinking worsened to the point where his wife left him in 1798 shortly after the birth of their fourth child. Apparently his drunken abuse of his wife included striking her with the flat of his sword. A few years later he broke an ankle that caused him to limp the rest of his life and he started to lose his eyesight. He managed to support himself through farm income and a half-pension from the British government.

Girty made a brief comeback in August of 1812. At the beginning of the War of 1812 the American army at Detroit surrendered to the British. Soon afterwards, Girty was seen on the streets of Detroit drunkenly boasting "here's old Simon Girty on American soil again." But a year later, the situation had changed, and with the Americans poised for an invasion of Canada, Girty fled to eastern Ontario, where he remained for three years.

When he returned he was completely blind and in failing health. Facing death, he quit drinking and his wife rejoined him in his final months. Simon Girty died on his farm on February 18, 1818. It was a peaceful end to a violent life.

CHAPTER FOUR

David Williamson and Hugh McGary

"Savage miscreants"

It has been said that history is written by the winners, so it should not be surprising that those labeled scoundrels and rogues tend to be those who chose the losing side. But it is important to note that some on the winning side still behaved badly. Some otherwise undistinguished leaders pop up briefly in history to illustrate this.

The American Revolution in the west was fought on two fronts, each of which offered an example of this. On the Pittsburgh front, David Williamson led a militia expedition that murdered 90 Christianized Indians. On the Kentucky front, Hugh McGary's wounded pride led to a disastrous defeat. Both men's actions in 1782 resulted in misguided revenges that took more innocent lives and perpetuated the injustices that often pervaded the frontier. Both were brave men serving a noble cause, but whose leadership resulted in disaster.

In the case of David Williamson, more is known about his victims than about himself, as the Moravian missionaries were better known and kept better records than the settlers who were flooding to western Pennsylvania in the late 18th Century. It is known that Williamson was born near Carlisle, Pennsylvania in 1752 and that his father's name was John. When he was just thirteen he went on a hunting and trapping trip to the Pittsburgh area and fell in love with the west. He persuaded his father and uncle Joseph to move their families to the frontier and they settled on Buffalo Creek in Donegal Township, Washington County. Their new home was just twelve miles from the Ohio River, between present day Washington, Pennsylvania, and Bethany, West Virginia.

This was far enough on the fringe of western settlement that it was among the first areas to be hit by Indian raiding parties who specialized in terrorizing individual homes. To combat what has been called "the war in the dooryard," settlers could connect their homes by a common stockade wall. These crude forts were called stations and were usually named after a local leader. By 1776, Williamson had established a station that included a triple cabin and springhouse. This station was never attacked, but many in the area were, and as a station leader, Williamson came to play a prominent role in frontier defense. Popular with the rank and file, he became a battalion commander in the Washington County militia.

Caught in the midst of the conflict between the Americans around Pittsburgh and the British and Indians near Detroit was a group of Christian Indians in the Tuscarawas Valley. Mainly members of the Delaware tribe, they had been converted by the Moravian missionaries who lived among them. The Moravians were originally from Central Europe and had come to America by way of England. They established a successful mission program working with Indians, stressing education and pacifism. By living with them, they earned the Indians' trust and respect and were often used as diplomatic intermediaries.

Being caught between two disparate cultures proved to be risky. Whites in particular were distrustful of all Indians, and the Moravians and their converts had to keep moving westward. In 1772 they were in western Pennsylvania when they were invited by the Delaware to join them in their villages along the Tuscarawas River. Led by missionaries David Zeisberger and John Heckewelder, they relocated beyond the reach of white settlement.

Here they thrived, with the mission towns of Schoenbrunn and Gnadenhutten doing particularly well. At Schoenbrunn, over 400 converts lived among 60 buildings that included a church that seated 100 and featured stained glass and a bell. The Moravians also built a school and published a Delaware language dictionary and speller, though in church they prayed in Delaware, preached in English, and sang hymns in German. Aided by the first prohibition laws west of the Alleghenies, the sober Moravian Indians flourished and became known for always having plenty of food stowed away.

But the ways of war soon engulfed this paradise. British and Americans both sought alliances with the various tribes of the Ohio country. Most Indians sided with the British, though the Delaware remained neutral due in large part to the influence of the Moravian missionaries. But it was difficult to remain neutral when living between two worlds in both a physical and cultural sense.

Indian raiding parties regularly stopped at the mission towns on their way to attack white settlers. Indian protocol dictated that the guests be fed, and as Heckewelder wrote "the quickest way to get rid of all warriors is to give them meals, which is all they want, and to refuse them would be folly, as then they would shoot cattle, and destroy the corn in the fields." But if they were hospitable to raiding parties, the Moravians also offered valuable services to the Americans. They regularly sent messengers out with warnings about the raiders and kept the commanders at Fort Pitt supplied with intelligence on all Indian movements.

Colonel John Gibson of the American army wrote "the Moravians have always given us the most convincing proofs of their attachment to the cause of America." Colonel Daniel Brodhead, in command at Fort Pitt, conceded, "it must be confessed that those good people at Coshocton have rendered the state much real service." In return for this information Heckewelder asked of Brodhead "all I request is not to let an Indian know a word of what I wrote."

But the non-Christian Delaware gradually came to favor the side of the British. In April of 1781 Brodhead launched a pre-emptive strike on the Delaware capital of Coshocton that included killing fifteen captives who had already surrendered. The Delaware then moved to the Sandusky region, which left the Moravian converts as the only Indians between Lake Erie and Pittsburgh. Without their fellow tribesmen as a buffer they were completely isolated.

Late that summer, a Wyandot war party stopped by for a free meal en route to an attack on Wheeling. The Moravians sent out a warning that foiled the surprise of the attack but one of the whites captured told of the Moravian warning. In response to this, a large Wyandot party came to the mission towns in September and demanded the converts accompany them to protective custody near Upper Sandusky. They were treated harshly on their forced journey and the white missionaries were sent to Detroit to face charges of treason.

A small group of converts led by missionary John Bull was permitted in November to return to retrieve unharvested corn. While at Gnadenhutten they encountered a militia party that may have included Williamson and who offered to take them to Pittsburgh, an offer that was eagerly accepted. Meanwhile, the other missionaries who were taken to Detroit were treated well and released. But the entire group spent a bleak and hungry winter until early in March when 90 men, women, and children were permitted to return to the Tuscarawas towns to finish retrieving the corn crop.

Normally the Indian braves of the hostile tribes didn't begin their raids until April, but in 1782 they were active in February, which greatly alarmed the western Pennsylvanians who feared it would be a bad year. Many of these settlers had already lost loved ones in attacks, and they were eager to avenge any raids. The year's activities began with the capture near Williamson's Station of a man named Carpenter. Having heard that Indians always burn the first captive of the year, Carpenter was fortunate enough to escape before being a part of such opening day festivities. He reported that two of the Indians that treated him most roughly spoke "Dutch," meaning German, and implying they were backsliding Moravians. Why two Indians most likely from the same tribe would converse in a European language not native to either was a question no one asked.

On February 10, a settler named Robert Wallace returned to find his home destroyed and his wife and children missing. These incidents resulted in the calling out of the county militia, which was to meet at Mingo Bottom on the Ohio below current Steubenville. Their destination would be the Moravian towns, as raiding parties still used the abandoned buildings as a way station and they hoped to catch them there.

But the waters of the Ohio were cold and high, and many of the mounted militiamen were reluctant to cross over. Finally, about 160 of them did make an attempt, with some horses being drowned in the process. At Mingo Bottom, they selected Williamson as their commander. This was probably done by election, although the exact details are not known.

On the way to the mission towns, the militia found the mutilated body of Mrs. Wallace, which further inflamed their rage against Indians. When they arrived at the outskirts of Gnadenhutten they encountered a lone Indian, who they shot so he wouldn't warn the others. The victim turned out to be Joseph Bull, son of the missionary John Bull and a Delaware mother. He was the only person in the campaign to die by gunshot.

The militia entered the town, and were greeted by families that were happy to see them. The Moravians readily surrendered their arms when the militia promised to take them to Pittsburgh, as they preferred the protective custody of the Americans. But Williamson's men did not keep their promises. They found Mrs. Wallace's dress in the town, and this may have hardened their feelings that the Moravians were at the very least dealing with the raiders. Also, with the raiders gone and safely into Indian territory, the militia was now likely to return home bereft of Indian scalps, so they turned to murder to salvage their pride.

Some accounts say Williamson disapproved of killing the captives but if he did he wasn't willing to exert any leadership on behalf of his beliefs. An early historian who interviewed Williamson's contemporaries concluded that, "His only fault was that of too easy a compliance with popular opinion and popular prejudice." Preferring to maintain his popularity, he put the matter to a vote. The first recorded vote on Ohio soil did no honor to the future state, as only eighteen men voted to show mercy. The other 88% of this electorate voted to commit mass murder of all their captives. The converts were informed that their destination was to be eternity rather than Pittsburgh, and they spent their last night singing hymns and praying.

On the morning of March 8, the captives were separated into two sheds designated as human slaughterhouses. The 29 men, 27 women, and 34 children were brought out in groups of two or three and executed by being struck with a cooper's mallet. After one soldier had killed about 20 people this way, he claimed fatigue and passed the hammer along, saying, "I think I have done pretty well for myself." After the mass murder was completed, the Indians were scalped for trophy purposes, and the bodies and the entire town were burned. Some have said the Gnadenhutten Massacre was a crime of passion, but the methodical way the militia set out to perform genocide was deliberate and dispassionate.

Williamson's men then returned home in triumph, proudly displaying their scalps. This encouraged more anti-Indian acts, and a group attacked some Delaware living on an island near Fort Pitt who were not only pro-American but in the service of the army. Colonel John Gibson, who had called Williamson's men "the most savage miscreants that ever degraded mankind" was himself openly threatened with scalping.

There were no printing presses in Pittsburgh until 1786, but as word began to filter to the papers back east, it became apparent that the killings were not something to be proud of. A lawyer for the Moravians wrote to Congress requesting an investigation, and concluded his plea by saying, "The tragic scenes of erecting two butcher houses or sheds and killing in cold blood ninety five brown or tawny sheep of Jesus Christ, one by one, is certainly taken notice of by the Shepherd, their Creator and Redeemer."

A member of the Pennsylvania Executive Council investigated and wrote to the governor "that affair is a subject of great speculation here—some condemning, others applauding the measure: but the accounts are so various that it is… impossible to ascertain the real truth. No person can give intelligence but those that were along… yet they will say nothing." Another citizen wrote the governor, "the better part of the community are of the opinion the perpetrators of that wicked deed ought to be brought to condign punishment; that without something is done by the government in the matter, it will disgrace the annals of the United States, and be an everlasting plea and cover for British cruelty."

But the investigation went nowhere, due in large part to stonewalling by General William Irvine, the American commander at Fort Pitt. Irvine's predecessor, Daniel Brodhead, had been removed after over 400 western Pennsylvanians signed a letter protesting his arbitrary and corrupt behavior, so Irvine was acutely aware that he needed local cooperation to prosecute the federal war effort. He wrote to the governor, "It will be almost impossible to obtain a just account of the conduct of the militia at Muskingum. No man can give any account except some of the party themselves; if therefore, an inquiry should appear serious, they are not obliged nor will they give evidence. For this and other reasons, I am of opinion further inquiry into the matter will not only be fruitless, but, in the end, may be attached with disagreeable consequence."

In a letter to his wife, Irvine was even more blunt. After describing how the militia "in cold blood... fell on them while they were singing hymns" and "did not spare either age or sex," he amazingly says he refuses to pass judgment. After mentioning how Gibson has lost standing by speaking out, he cautions his wife "you will keep your mind to yourself" and concludes with a perverse pride that, "No man knows whether I approve or disapprove of killing the Moravians."

The Indian tribes of Ohio were united in outrage over the killings and swore vengeance. When a larger militia contingent invaded Ohio in May they believed that the purpose was to finish off the Christian Indians. The real goal of this follow-up mission was to go farther than ever into Indian territory to wipe out the war making towns of the Sandusky area. The federal troops at Fort Pitt were too few and too poorly supplied to be of any use, so this was to be a mounted militia campaign.

Irvine wrote to George Washington on May 21, 1782, "As they will elect their own officers, I have taken some pains to get Colonel Crawford appointed to command and hope he will be." He added that the militia "pressed me for some officers. I have sent them Lieutenant Rose, my aid-de-camp... and a surgeon. These two are all I could venture to spare." Crawford was an experienced officer and long-time personal friend of Washington's. Rose was really Baron Gustavas de Rosenthal, a Russian nobleman who had fled to America after killing a man in a duel, and the surgeon was Dr. John Knight.

When the militia assembled at Mingo Bottom on May 24, Williamson again played a prominent role in an election. Parlaying his recent success to exploit his popularity, Williamson ran a strong race, but narrowly lost to Crawford by 235 votes to 230. Rose wrote to Irvine that Williamson was gracious in defeat. "Colonels Williamson and Crawford did seem to have numerous and obstinate adherents. The latter carried the election this day by five votes; and I cannot but give Colonel Williamson the utmost credit for his exhorting the whole to be unanimous... and cheerfully submitted to being second in command. I think if it had been otherwise... very likely we should have dispersed."

It would have been better if they had dispersed. After being watched all the way, this force was attacked near Upper Sandusky on June 4. A daylong battle was a standoff, but the next day the British and Indians got reinforcements. With the possibility of being surrounded looming, Crawford ordered a retreat, and in the confusion, a small group, including himself and Dr. Knight, became separated from the main body. Williamson assumed command during the generally orderly retreat. Upon returning, he wrote a brief report to Irvine, which was proper protocol. This terse note was proof that Williamson could write, yet no official report of the Gnadenhutten expedition has been found.

Lieutenant Rose also wrote a report and later penned an extended account of the expedition. A better writer in

English than most of the militia, he gave this candid assessment of Williamson, " Williamson is brave as Caesar and active but... fond of thrusting himself in danger, he leaves everything else to chance. He... is quite ignorant how to dispose of men, or how to fight them to advantage. He knows too well how high he is in the opinion of the people and among these he takes upon himself the airs of a man of consequence. However, he is open to advice and instructions. His oratory is suited to the taste of the people his countrymen, and their bigoted notions stand him in lieu of arguments."

A few weeks later, a disheveled and distraught Dr. Knight staggered into Fort Pitt after escaping Indian captivity. He gave a detailed account of witnessing Crawford's slow death by torture that was their revenge for Gnadenhutten. Just as Williamson had wanted warriors' scalps but would settle for ones from Christian Indians, the tribes would have preferred to torture Williamson to death but would settle for Crawford. Thus the innocent continued to die for the sins of the guilty, as the war in the west wound down.

The Gnadenhutten Massacre did accomplish the rare feat of shaming the Americans into offering compensation. After independence had been won Congress offered the Moravians land grants on the site of their old villages. But these lands were part of the newly created Northwest Territory and had to be surveyed first. En route to Marietta in 1788 to lobby for speedy surveying, John Heckewelder had a chance meeting with Williamson. After hearing his fellow traveler's name, Heckewelder "suspected at once that this was the notorious Colonel Williamson who had seized our Indians on the Muskingum. I asked him further if he had ever been beyond the Ohio and whether the land there was really as good as it was said to be. He said it was much too good for its present inhabitants." The mild-mannered Heckewelder did not confront Williamson, but wrote, "many a curse was sent after him by those who knew who he was."

Williamson remained popular with his neighbors, and after the Revolution he was elected Sheriff of Washington County. Ironically, the downfall of this massacre leader was that he was too accommodating. He was known to be lenient with lawbreakers and in giving security he eventually lost his extensive land holdings. Unable to properly provide for his family, he died in poverty in 1809. His main claim to fame was a brief appearance in history as the leader at an atrocity, where he was not so much malicious but was a part of a lax and pandering leadership cadre.

Hugh McGary's leadership style was anything but lax. Aggressive and hot-tempered, he had a decisive demeanor that was representative of the rugged pioneers who settled Kentucky. But while he was undoubtedly brave, his lack of critical thinking skills and impetuousness were a major contributing factor in one of the worst defeats in the state's history.

The rich soils of Kentucky had been coveted ever since rumors of them had reached white men. A young Daniel Boone had first heard about them while serving with Braddock's army in the French and Indian War. But this fabled land was beyond the area where white men were permitted to settle by the King's Proclamation of 1763. It wasn't until 1768 that it became safe to explore this area.

Boone first visited Kentucky the next year and found that the land was every bit as good as had been described. But it wasn't until the Shawnee had been defeated in battle at

Point Pleasant in 1774 that permanent settlement could be attempted. The next year a flood of immigrants living on the previous western fringes of civilization began crossing the mountains.

Hugh McGary was among the first to make this move. Born in 1744 in Augusta County, Virginia, he had grown up on what was then the frontier. The son of John and Sarah McGary, he had little formal education, but acquired a rudimentary literacy. In 1763, he moved to the Yadkin Valley of North Carolina, where Daniel Boone was a neighbor. In 1767, he married Mary Buntin Ray, a widow with three sons under the age of six. Restless and not owning land, McGary was a likely candidate for a western exodus.

In the spring of 1775, McGary joined a group of men led by James Harrod, who had already surveyed and laid out a town site. Arriving by way of the Cumberland Gap, this group planted a corn crop, a sign of legitimacy and intended permanency. They then returned east for the summer. That fall McGary and Boone and four other men returned with their wives and families. Arriving on September 8, these were the first families to settle in Kentucky.

These pioneers had launched their venture at an inauspicious time. The outbreak of the American Revolution that year had thrown the country into turmoil and the British at Detroit were eager to supply and encourage raids by Indians who resented the new settlers. And the Kentuckians were in a sort of legal limbo, as they weren't really a part of the thirteen colonies. But as the land they occupied had been claimed by Virginia, they sought protection from that state.

On June 6, 1776, representatives from Harrodsburg, Boonesborough and St. Asaphs elected George Rogers Clark and John Jones as their delegates to the Virginia legislature.

After a hazardous journey, they found they had no official status until Virginia created Kentucky County in December. McGary, who had claimed over 400 acres of land at Shawnee Spring near the Harrodsburg settlement, assumed a prominent role in the new county. On February 27, 1777, he was named Chairman of the Committee of Safety for the region. He immediately wrote to Governor Patrick Henry requesting he "devise some method to guard us against the attacks of our merciless enemy."

His plea was brought home in a personal way just a week later. Two of McGary's stepsons were caught outside the fort's gate by an Indian raiding party, and only one made it back to the fort. The immediate reaction of the volatile McGary was to berate James Harrod for lapses in the fort's defenses. The two men engaged in a loud argument and actually pointed guns at each other until Mrs. McGary turned her husband's weapon away and beseeched them to look for her son's body.

This was just one of many Indian raids on the isolated Kentucky settlements. With no federal help available and not much aid from Virginia, the settlers formed their own county militia to provide for their defense. McGary became an officer in his local unit. He was also entrusted by Clark, the overall military commander, to travel to Fort Pitt conveying information in 1777.

McGary withdrew from civic activity in the spring of 1780 when his wife died and left him to care for at least a half dozen children. In August, however, he remarried 22-year-old Catherine "Catsey" Yocum, with whom he had several more children. He re-entered militia service at a time when the increasing number of Kentucky settlements were becoming even more frequent targets of raids.

In the spring of 1780, two Kentucky forts had surrendered when faced with a raiding party that included British artillery capable of battering the surrounded fort's walls. To counter this threat, Clark organized a raid that included a cannon and headed for Shawnee country. McGary went on this expedition as a captain. On the march north, he led an unauthorized hunting party into an ambush where nine of his men were killed. On August 8, Clark's force destroyed the Indian town of Piqua, near present-day Springfield, which halted raiding for a while.

As the Kentucky settlements continued to grow, the region was divided into three counties. In the newly created Lincoln County, McGary was made a member of the county court and a major in the militia. The contentious Kentuckians were a litigious lot, and McGary wound up spending considerable time in court as a justice, witness, and defendant. But he achieved his greatest notoriety for his role in the Battle of Blue Licks.

In August of 1782, a large raiding party that included Indians and renegades such as Simon Girty and Andrew McKee attacked central Kentucky. After briefly surrounding Bryant's Station near present-day Lexington on August 16, they killed livestock and burned crops and withdrew before reinforcements could arrive at the fort. This was a normal pattern for raiding parties and the usual response of the Kentuckians was to gather militia and follow to try to recapture prisoners. But the scattered militia was hard to bring together. If the settlers left immediately they might not have enough men to challenge the raiders; but if they waited until their numbers were sufficient, the raiders might already be safely across the Ohio.

On this occasion, McGary advocated waiting until a large contingent under Colonel Benjamin Logan arrived. His suggestion was derisively dismissed in a way that McGary felt questioned his bravery. The 182 available men under Colonel John Todd moved out and found the raiders' trail surprisingly easy to follow. On August 19, they found an enemy force leisurely camped just across the Licking River near a ford on a horseshoe bend.

Daniel Boone, a ranking member of the militia, suspected a trap. He had reason to be wary of the Blue Licks, as he had been captured by Indians here four years earlier while serving as a hunter for an expedition that was boiling brine to make salt for meat preservation. Boone had agreed to lead the Indians to the salt makers if they promised not to attack Boonesborough, which he felt could not hold out against such a large force. Boone later escaped, but the lawsuit-loving Kentuckians then court marshaled their biggest folk hero for leading Indians to the salt makers, although he was completely exonerated.

While Boone pointed out it was a perfect spot for an ambush, McGary pressed for an immediate attack. According to some accounts, he shouted, "All men who are not cowards follow me!" and waded into the river to lead an unauthorized charge. But the men who accused McGary of "vain and seditious expressions" were not at the battle, and it appears that the officers actually consulted and scouted before advancing.

But there is no doubt that McGary agitated for action to his fellow officers and he didn't hesitate to throw questions of their courage back in their faces. After having their manhood so questioned, the Kentuckians crossed the river and marched into a withering fire from a well-planned ambush. Within fifteen minutes they had 70 men killed before they could get back across the river. Among the dead were Colonel Todd, another colonel, a major, and four captains. Boone survived, but his teenage son Israel was killed, a loss for which Boone never forgave himself. McGary escaped without a scratch.

It was the worst loss suffered by the Kentuckians in the war. When they returned to the battlefield with Logan's force, they found 43 corpses so brutally mutilated that not a single one could be identified. In the aftermath of the battle, Boone blamed himself for allowing his instincts to be overruled. McGary, however, acted as he had when his stepson had been killed and looked for someone to blame. He faulted Colonel Todd for not waiting for Logan and implied that Todd did not want to surrender overall command to Logan. This was a charge Todd could not refute since he had been killed in the battle.

Though few men blamed McGary openly for the disaster, there was enough of an undercurrent that McGary felt obligated to address it. Nine days after the battle he wrote to Logan, "I suppose you heard of my bad conduct" and insisting "if you think I am faulty I should be fond to have a hearing in the matter." But no official investigation was ever conducted, and with the death of so many high-ranking officers, McGary actually rose in stature as he performed colonel's duties in counter raids that fall.

The war was all but over in November of 1782, when Clark led another foray into Indian country north of the Ohio. With over 1,000 men he got as far north as present-day Fort Loramie, where they destroyed a trading post that had been used to supply raiding parties. They laid waste to other

Indian villages as well, and McGary was the leader of a 500-member party that conducted some of these raids.

But McGary began to play a lesser role as peacetime approached. One of the reasons for this was his conviction in April of 1783 for gambling on horse races. This is no crime in Kentucky today, but then the court ruled that "Hugh McGary, gentleman, be deemed an infamous gambler and that he shall not be eligible to any office of trust or honor within this state." When Virginia created additional new countries that year McGary was passed over for both judicial and militia posts.

Over the next four years, the Kentuckians devoted their efforts to future governance. All were dissatisfied in being under the control of the eastern Virginian government. Some sought to form a new state, while others talked of an independent nation. At a series of conferences the citizens discussed the Spanish control of the Mississippi and British encouragement of Indian war parties.

Indian raids were still a problem for Kentucky residents. At Fort Finney at the mouth of the Great Miami, the Shawnee in 1786 had accepted harsh terms that allowed for white settlement. But Indian raids continued, although most came from the Miami tribe in southern Indiana. In the fall of 1786 the Kentuckians sent two forces out to strike at the Indians. One group under Clark was to attack the Miami while another under Logan would chastise the Ohio Shawnee.

McGary was back in good graces by now, and on September 5 he was promoted to Lieutenant Colonel and sent on Logan's expedition. On his third raid into Ohio, McGary and his men encountered no hostile bands of warriors, but they did destroy lots of villages and crops. On

October 6 they attacked the village of the aged chief Moluntha, near present-day West Liberty. Moluntha had not only signed and supported the Fort Finney Treaty, but he proudly flew an American flag above his village, which unfortunately did not protect it from Americans.

Logan had earlier given orders not to harm Indian prisoners. This was because at Piqua in 1780 a cousin of Clark's who had been taken captive was killed when attempting to rejoin the Kentuckians while dressed as an Indian. But Logan rescinded this order when he feared it might give his men less of an edge, and McGary took advantage of this change. As Moluntha was speaking with his captors, McGary burst in and demanded to know if Moluntha had been at Blue Licks. Moluntha, who probably didn't understand the question, smiled and nodded. McGary then grabbed a small ax and buried it in the chief's skull, killing him instantly.

In the pandemonium that followed, McGary was seized by a Colonel Trotter and several others who were outraged by his conduct. McGary countered profanely that he would kill Trotter or anyone else who tried to stop him from killing Indians when he wanted. Some wanted to try McGary on the spot, but Logan insisted for McGary's protection that they return home first. McGary's barbarity not only stirred up all Indians, but it upset the commander of the United States Army that was trying to preserve peace. Colonel Josiah Harmar was critical of the entire raid and particularly of the murder of Moluntha, who, he said, "had always been represented as a friend of the United States."

On March 20, 1787, McGary's court martial was held at Bardstown. He also filed countercharges against Trotter for unauthorized distribution of rum to the troops, but the charges against McGary were more serious. He was accused of murder, disobeying the order not to harm captives, use of abusive and threatening language, and conduct unbecoming an officer. He was acquitted of disobeying orders since Logan had rescinded that order, but was convicted on the other counts. For murdering an unarmed man and threatening another officer he was sentenced to be suspended from the militia for one year. After this slap on the wrist, he resumed his career as landholder and judge and was even elected county sheriff.

In 1790, McGary made a trip to Natchez. Traveling in his party was a young Nashville lawyer named Andrew Jackson and his wife Rachel. But Rachel had already been married to Lawrence Robards, who was an acquaintance of McGary's. The two had a brief unhappy marriage before separating, but at the time, divorce was so rare it could only be obtained by petitioning the legislature for permission to file. Robards did this, but the trial was not held until September 1793. At this time, McGary appeared as a paid witness for Robards and testified that Rachel had presented herself as another man's wife, and the divorce was granted on grounds of adultery.

This trial erupted into a national scandal 34 years later when Jackson was running for President. An enterprising reporter uncovered the story that the potential first lady was a bigamist and the candidate therefore an adulterer. Jackson's supporters accused McGary of perjury over twenty years after his death, but it appears his account was an honest one. Jackson went on to survive the scandal and win the election, but Rachel died before she could become first lady.

In 1795, McGary left his farm at Shawnee Spring and moved into Harrodsburg to operate a tavern. This didn't last long and he wound up around 1800 living in Henderson, Kentucky, on the Ohio River. Here he operated both a tavern and a tannery. Although he had prospered as a businessman, McGary overreached and got into trouble.

According to a county history, he was the first man in Henderson County to be convicted of selling liquor without a license. He faced more serious problems on April 21, 1803 when he was charged with stealing a large sum of money from the saddlebags of a tavern guest. The Kentuckians were tolerant of crimes involving horse racing and whiskey, and they could even forgive the killing of an unarmed Indian. But theft was a serious charge and according to one contemporary "public sentiment seemed to be against the Colonel."

The disposition of this case is not known, as a flood destroyed courthouse records. But not long afterwards, McGary left Kentucky, and moved across the Ohio to Indiana Territory. Catsey died in 1804, but he remarried that same year and fathered two more daughters while in his 60s.

McGary had owned as many as fourteen slaves at one time, but slavery was illegal north of the Ohio. To rectify this, he freed his slaves and then signed them to long-term indentured servant contracts. These servants were supposed to be free after their contacts expired, but apparently some of them were later resold. But this crime was perpetuated by his heirs, as McGary died in Indiana in 1806. He achieved a brief posthumous notoriety in 1827 during Jackson's presidential campaign, but today he is chiefly known for his vocal role in a bitter defeat and a misguided attempt to avenge that defeat.

Outline of a blockhouse site at Fort Pitt with the Pittsburgh skyline in the background. For over 35 years, this was the place where the west began for most frontier adventurers.

Monument in Wyandot County, Ohio noting where Colonel William Crawford was tortured to death and Simon Girty cemented his reputation.

Marker at Gnadenhutten, Ohio, where nearly 100 Christian Indians were methodically murdered in 1782.

Monument in Nicholas County, Kentucky, for 70 men killed in 15 minutes at Blue Licks in 1782.

Re-interred remains of Lewis Wetzel in family cemetery in Marshall County, West Virginia.

William Wells translates for his surrogate fathers Little Turtle and Anthony Wayne in Howard Chandler Christy's painting The Signing of the Treaty of GreeneVille that is displayed at the Ohio State Capitol (courtesy Ohio Historical Society).

The rebuilt Blennerhassett mansion is a West Virginia State Park today.

Harman Blennerhassett, the ineffectual intellectual who met disaster through his involvement with the Burr Conspiracy (courtesy Blennerhassett Island Historical State Park).

CHAPTER FIVE

Lewis Wetzel and Samuel Mason

"Something ferocious in his look"

Lewis Wetzel and Samuel Mason may seem on the surface to be an odd pairing. It's true that they both bravely served in the defense of the Wheeling area from Indian attacks during the American Revolution, and they both died in the Natchez area at about the same time after running afoul of the law in their later years. And it's certainly true that both were frontier legends featured in numerous fantastic escapades despite a paucity of verifiable facts. But the two men are a unique pairing because their contrasts are even more striking than their similarities.

Wetzel was an illiterate but forthright woodsman who killed Indians, while Mason was the smooth talking head of a criminal operation. Mason boasted that he had never killed, but his henchmen robbed and killed at will, and Mason is properly reviled today. Wetzel was as honest as they come, yet he went to prison for a non-violent white collar crime, and is widely considered a hero today, despite having personally killed dozens of men.

It would be wrong to categorize Lewis Wetzel as a scoundrel, even if by today's standards he would be considered a racist serial killer. His unsurpassed skills as a scout helped make the frontier safe and his hatred of Indians must be viewed in the context of his times. Wetzel could be called a spy, for that term was often used to describe the scouts who went into the woods alone to gather intelligence about Indian activity. However, modern connotations of spying imply some sort of duplicity, and no one was more open and less deceitful than Wetzel. But if you define rogue as a solitary creature who operates outside of the normal controls, then Wetzel was the quintessential rogue. Lewis Wetzel lived by his own code and never compromised it.

The problem with talking about such a legendary rogue is that there are so few facts to go with the abundance of legend. Wetzel stealthily avoided history's radar in several ways. He never learned to write so he left no papers. He never married, had children, or owned any property. And he rarely joined organized military expeditions, preferring to operate in the woods on his own.

He did not boast of his exploits in conversation either, but at least his grateful neighbors could go on record on his behalf. In an unsuccessful petition to obtain Revolutionary War pensions for the family, neighbors claimed that the Wetzels "during the period of war aforesaid, rendered more service and protection to the frontier than any family then living on it." These neighbors also passed on a body of embellished legends that will have to serve in describing Wetzel in the absence of facts.

It has been established that Lewis Wetzel was born in August of 1763, the fourth of seven children of John and Mary Wetzel. The Wetzels were of Swiss extraction but came to America via Holland around 1733. They moved around on the frontier, and John married a neighbor girl named Mary Bonnet in 1756. The family lived at times in Virginia, Maryland, and Pennsylvania, and it is believed that Lewis was born in Lancaster County, Pennsylvania.

In 1770 the family moved west to the new settlement of Wheeling on the Ohio River, and it was here that young Lewis roamed as a child, and honed his unerring wilderness instincts. The Ohio River was the dividing line between white and Indian territory, which meant that the isolated post at Wheeling was often the first place to be attacked, which tested the mettle of the Zanes, Wetzels, and McCulloughs who pioneered here.

Ruthless Indian raiding parties besieged Wheeling's Fort Henry three times during the Revolution, which contributed to a widespread hatred of all Indians among the settlers. One man defended his killing of Indian children simply by saying "nits make lice." Hardly a frontier family was untouched by these raids. In fact, of the six males in the Wetzel family, all six were captured or killed by Indians during the ten-year period from 1777-1786. In three cases the captivities were brief, but Martin was held for three years, and George and John Sr. were killed in separate incidents along the Ohio.

Lewis was the first to be captured, when he was just thirteen. In April of 1777 Indians were reported in the area and most settlers "forted up" in nearby stockades. But as it was planting season, John Wetzel sent Lewis and his eleven-year-old brother Jacob back to work briefly at putting in a corn crop. One morning they were ambushed and Lewis was wounded and both boys captured. They were hurried across the Ohio towards Indian country.

On their second night as captives, the boys were able to loosen their bonds and sneak out of camp. But they had no shoes, so Lewis crept back among the sleeping Indians to retrieve two pairs of moccasins. Then he noiselessly went back a third time to retrieve his father's rifle for protection on their return. They were pursued but managed to elude their captors and make it back to the Ohio. The wounded Lewis was too weak to swim across, so the brothers grabbed driftwood and floated over, taking care to keep the rifle dry. The brothers were hailed as heroes upon their safe return and Lewis was praised for his coolness and daring.

Lewis Wetzel grew to manhood in this time and place of strife, and he perfected his woodland skills with this milieu in mind. As a man, Wetzel grew to be about five foot ten with broad shoulders and big arms. He had a dark complexion and a face that was marked by a bout with smallpox. He was taciturn and withdrawn in mixed company, though he might be coaxed into playing the fiddle for his friends. One of his predominant physical characteristics was his long hair that went down to his calves when let down, offering a tempting scalp for any Indian who dared to try and take it. His other unique feature was intense black eyes that were described by a contemporary as "piercing as the dagger's point."

Wetzel's physical abilities were also impressive. Not only was he the best shot and fastest runner around Wheeling, but he combined these two essential skills into his signature move. Loading a muzzle-loading rifle involved over twenty distinct movements, which made a rifleman vulnerable in the time it took to use powder, cartridge, ball and ramrod to reload. Wetzel trained himself to do this process while running with a long gait at full speed. He got so good at this that in a contest with Continental troops he was able to reload quicker on the run than the soldiers could standing still. Wetzel also became a master at silent wilderness tracking. When a neighbor boasted too loudly of his own woodland prowess, Wetzel successfully wagered that he could sneak up on him in an open field and touch him on the shoulder, and he even let his victim choose which shoulder.

These were publicly noted demonstrations of Wetzel's abilities, but his most significant work was done alone and in secret. Wetzel would usually go out alone and return with information about enemy movements as well as scalps. He seldom said much about these exploits, though he might laconically complain that "I treed four Indians, but one got away." Men who tried to keep up with Wetzel on these dangerous forays often failed to make it back. On example of this was John Madison, a cousin of James Madison, who was killed by Indians after hiring Wetzel as a guide.

Another example was a man named Mills, who convinced Wetzel to help him retrieve a horse he had to abandon near present-day St. Clairsville. They found the horse tied to a tree, which Wetzel knew was a trap but Mills fell for it and was killed by four Indians. Wetzel killed one and began running and reloading before turning and shooting his nearest pursuer. He did this again and continued until the last Indian abandoned the chase of a man whose Gun Was Always Loaded.

On another occasion Wetzel accompanied a large party that offered a cash prize for the first Indian scalp collected. However, this group discovered a much larger Indian force nearby and decided to retreat. But Wetzel refused to leave, and insisted on remaining until he got his scalp, and collected the bounty.

There are many more versions of unconfirmed Wetzel tales, some of which are clearly fanciful. One story that is probably true concerns an Indian who lurked near the fort and imitated a turkey's call. Hunters would be lured into ambush by this decoy, until Wetzel put an end to it by patiently stalking and ambushing the ambusher. In an exaggerated version of this story, he even anonymously saves his widowed mother's new beau in the process. There are also several versions of a tale of Wetzel helping a young man rescue his fiancé from Indians, with the most reliable story about a woman named Rose Forrest. And there are tales of Wetzel putting his hat on a stick to draw Indian fire and using all sorts of stratagems to foil hapless Indians. In none of these tales does Wetzel ever torture or take delight in the suffering of any Indian. But in nearly all of them he kills adult male Indian braves. No one knows how many Indians Wetzel killed, with estimates ranging from merely a few dozen to up to a hundred.

This was not always a good thing, even in times of war. In 1782, the sixteen-year-old Wetzel accompanied a military party under Colonel Daniel Brodhead, one of the few times Wetzel's name shows up on militia muster rolls. This force destroyed the principle Delaware town at Coshocton and killed several warriors, including some who had already surrendered. After the fighting, a chief was talking to Brodhead, when allegedly "a man named Wetzel" approached and suddenly killed the chief with a tomahawk.

Some versions claim it was Martin Wetzel who did the killing, but he was not on this particular expedition. Other accounts maintain it was Lewis and some just said it was a Wetzel. Brodhead made no official report on the matter, so it's entirely possible it never happened at all. There were plenty of other Indian murders to get this one confused with, as the Delaware White Eyes and the Shawnees Cornstalk and Moluntha were all friendly chiefs who were murdered while in American custody during this period.

If Wetzel did not perform this deed, there would be future incidents in times of peace where his need to kill Indians would get him in trouble. The British and Indian attack on Fort Henry in September 1782 has been called the last battle of the American Revolution. But the formal end of the war did not mean an end to Indian raids, so Wetzel's services as a scout were still in demand for the next several years. But with the establishment of the Northwest Territory in 1787, the new United States government decided to employ peaceful means to establish settlements across the Ohio River. At the treaty of Fort Harmar at the mouth of the Muskingum in 1789, the Americans purchased settlement rights from various tribes.

In such a climate, killing Indians was no longer desirable, but Wetzel couldn't help himself. In July of 1789, he and a companion traveled to the Fort Harmar area apparently for the express purpose of killing Indians. They managed to find a victim easily enough and shot him in an ambush, but there were two unique things about the shooting. One was that the victim was not an enemy combatant, but a sometime-contract federal employee who had been used as a messenger during treaty negotiations. The other was that in this shooting the victim survived and filed a complaint.

On July 9, 1789 the commander of Fort Harmar, General Josiah Harmar wrote to Secretary of War Henry Knox that "a trusty confidential Indian was wounded by some vagabond whites from the neighborhood of Wheeling.... The villain who wounded him I am informed was one Lewis Whitzell (sic). I am in hopes to be able to apprehend him and deliver him to Judge Parsons to be dealt with; but would much rather have it in my power to order such vagabonds hanged up immediately without trial."

Some accounts claim that Harmar sent a detachment of federal troops to Wheeling to arrest Wetzel but the troops were turned back by a populace that was outraged that a folk hero be arrested for merely shooting an Indian. While these sentiments were no doubt felt, there is no record of a military expedition, and Wetzel most likely was arrested while still in the area. Because the infant territorial capital at Marietta still had no jail, Wetzel was taken across the Muskingum and imprisoned at Fort Harmar.

He wasn't there long before he escaped. In the more colorful versions, he scampered up the fort's walls in handcuffs before the astonished garrison. He then hid along the Ohio River until he found a sympathetic settler who could remove his irons. Wetzel then proceeded down the Ohio but was recaptured in August at Limestone (present-day Maysville), Kentucky, when federal soldiers burst into the home where he was staying. He was then taken on to Cincinnati where the new Fort Washington was being built. But as his victim had by now recovered and left the area and citizens were protesting his incarceration, he was soon released for lack of evidence by Judge Symmes.

However, his recapture had implications relating to the new Constitution that had just taken effect. On September 10, 1789 the Frankfort-based *Kentucky Gazette* complained that "a free citizen of this country, in the house of his friend, in the peaceable pursuit of his business, is seized by a military officer at the head of his soldiers, taken into custody, confined and hurried… out of the reach of your laws—away from his friends into a military garrison." The outrage over the high-handed methods employed by the federal troops compelled Harmar to order a court martial. But after $20 taken from Wetzel was returned, the army's investigation of itself unsurprisingly ruled they had done nothing wrong.

Though now a free man, Wetzel began to look at new options. He still liked to take hunting trips with his fellow legend Simon Kenton, who was a close friend to his brother Jacob, but with peace looming Wetzel needed different adventures. He signed on as a flatboatman and headed down the Ohio and Mississippi Rivers. Wetzel was every bit as tough as other boatmen in this Mike Fink era, but he got in trouble with the Spanish authorities that controlled the area below Natchez.

After killing dozens of men without punishment, it was a strange irony that Wetzel was imprisoned for counterfeiting, a crime for which the illiterate woodsman had neither aptitude nor interest. While staying with a Spanish citizen, he either passed counterfeit currency or else took the fall for his host's activity, and was forced to spend two years in prison in New Orleans. He was finally released through American help and returned to Wheeling by way of Philadelphia. He stayed briefly, and those he saw noted that prison had been hard on the freedom-loving frontiersman. He soon left for the south again, possibly to gain revenge on his accuser.

He returned briefly once more, but spent the rest of his life on the lower Mississippi. He died twenty miles from Natchez in 1808 at the age of 44 from an unknown disease. Some stories have said he started out on the Lewis and Clark expedition and left after a few months, but there is no record of him in any official accounts. Considering that one of the missions of the expedition was to keep peace with the Indians, it may have been just as well that Wetzel was not along.

While Wetzel's body was in a modest grave in Mississippi, his stature continued to grow in the Ohio Valley, and Wetzel County, West Virginia was named for him. In 1942 his bones were re-interred in the family cemetery in Marshall County, West Virginia, among the people who still consider him their greatest folk hero.

A man who was in the Wheeling area about the same time provides an interesting contrast to Wetzel. Samuel Mason was a militia officer who served bravely in the defense of Fort Henry. But Mason wound up being the leader of a criminal empire comprising the most notorious band of thieves and murderers in the west, and his ultimate fate was said to have been his head turned in by former partners eager to collect the reward money.

Mason was born in Virginia around 1750 to a prominent family. One of Samuel Mason's brothers was married to a sister of Benjamin Harrison, who was a signer of the Declaration of Independence, and the father of a U.S. president and great grandfather of another.

Mason came west as a young man and settled in Ohio County near Wheeling. He joined the county militia at the onset of the American Revolution and rose to the rank of captain. In absence of regular troops on the frontier, the militia played a vital role in defense. General Edward Hand, the commander at Fort Pitt, sent Captain Mason on several missions pursuing raiding parties, and in August 1777, ordered him to Fort Henry in Wheeling. When the fort was attacked on September 1, Mason and his guard were caught outside the gates and 23 of 28 men were killed. Mason was seriously wounded, but managed to hide and avoid being captured. A report written about this time says of Mason, "This brave young man will no doubt meet a reward adequate to his merit."

Two of his brothers went on George Rogers Clark's expedition, but Mason remained at Fort Henry. He accompanied Colonel Daniel Brodhead's expedition to Iroquois country in 1779 and remained a militia officer throughout the war. In 1780 he also opened a tavern along Wheeling Creek two miles east of town. It is not known how well he prospered in this endeavor, but a series of horse thefts in the area led some to speculate that he was supplementing his income via illegal activities. Before anything concrete could come of these allegations, Mason moved further west.

He eventually wound up in Henderson, Kentucky, an Ohio River town across from present day Evansville, Indiana. As a literate patrician on the edge of the frontier, he soon rose to a position of prominence in his new community and was made a justice of the peace. With his wife, four sons, and a daughter, he briefly became a respectable civic leader. But he did seem to come into conflict with several other prominent citizens and in several cases his rivals wound up being beaten by unknown assailants.

Mason's conduct came out into the open in 1794 at the wedding party he threw for his daughter. He had previously disapproved of his prospective son-in-law, a smooth-talking tough named Kuykendall who was known to carry devil's claws, a virulent early form of brass knuckles that could tear a man's face up. But Mason suddenly changed his mind and threw the couple a grand party, and didn't even seem to mind when told of how Kuykendall had been smuggled into his home previously. But sometime in the course of the party, the groom stepped out and was never seen again.

This disappearance could not be explained and Mason and his wife had to flee just ahead of the law, a pattern that he often repeated. His first destination was Diamond Island, a robber's roost on the Ohio just fourteen miles downstream from Henderson. The thieves who dwelled here made a living preying on the flatboatmen who were then in their heyday on the Ohio and Mississippi Rivers. Pioneers and cargo were steadily heading down these rivers, and until the invention of the steamboat the traffic was almost all one way. Mason saw the lucrative potential of robbing these travelers.

Around 1797 he moved about 70 miles downstream to the location that came to be associated with him. Here on the Illinois side of the river was a large cave in a rock face that offered a long view of the river. This spot, known as Cave-in-Rock, was already used as a bandit's lair, but Mason moved in and took the whole operation to a new level. He made a sign advertising, "Wilson's Liquor Vault and House of Entertainment" and began to cater to the rough flatboat trade. There was no Wilson, but Mason adopted an old corporate trick of creating a persona for commercial purposes. The entertainment referred to consisted of gambling and prostitution, and Mason soon had a booming if disreputable business.

Not content merely to defraud his clientele, Mason branched out into robbing settlers who were not inclined to visit his establishment. His usual method was to place someone upstream claiming to be in distress and requesting a ride to Cave-in-Rock. Once there, the crew was overpowered and killed, and all goods stolen. Mason even found a way to prey on boats that he could not lure into his lair. If a particularly prosperous looking boat failed to stop he would send word to crews he had waiting further downstream. One man would approach the boat and offer to guide them through narrow channels and would pilot the crew into an ambush. The success of these operations attracted cutthroats from all over and Cave-in-Rock became a crowded den of thieves and river pirates.

The most famous villains who came here were the Harpe brothers, the most ruthless of frontier murderers. The Harpes were born in North Carolina—Micajah (Big) Harpe in 1768, and Wiley (Little) Harpe in 1770. Their father had been a Tory during the Revolution, and this made the family outcasts after the bitter civil wars of the period. While northern Tories often fled to Canada, in the south the best chance for a fresh start was to head west. The Harpes did this, arriving in the Knoxville area about 1795.

The group they traveled with was hardly a traditional family. The two brothers were accompanied by three women—two sisters, who were apparently attached to Big, and a preacher's daughter who was Little's mate. This odd clan tried regular farming for a while, but the Harpes soon discovered it was easier to steal hogs than raise them. They soon branched out into horse theft and arson and in 1798 they committed their first murder. They disposed of the body by cutting out the entrails, filling the body cavity with stones, and sinking it in a stream. This method was employed frequently thereafter, but in this case the body resurfaced and the Harpes had to flee.

The entire clan headed for Kentucky and financed their travels by robbing and killing other travelers. However they were caught and charged with murder in January 1799. While awaiting the trial it was discovered that all three Harpe women were pregnant, and they each delivered a baby in jail in successive months. But the proud fathers did not stick around, as they escaped from jail in March. The women were sympathetically acquitted and immediately rejoined the Harpes, who now had a $300 reward offered for their recapture.

The governor's wanted poster described the brothers thusly: "Micajah Harpe is about six feet high, of a robust make, and about 30 or 32 years of age. He has an ill-looking, downcast countenance, and his hair is black and short... Wiley Harpe is very meager in his face, has short black hair but not quite as curly as his brother's... and has likewise a downcast countenance."

After escaping, the Harpe brothers went on a killing spree that entered them into legendary status, with some claiming that their murders included over thirty victims in the next six months. They usually preyed on solo travelers but on one occasion they butchered a party of ten. Their most notorious killing was when they were hiding in a cave and Big Harpe became so upset at the crying of one of the babies that he dashed the child's brains on a rock. As their fame spread, the *Frankfort Palladium* opined on August 15, "we are happy to hear they are closely pursued and sincerely hope they will ere long meet the punishment which the atrocity of their crimes demands."

Being hotly pursued across Kentucky, the Harpes allegedly approached Cave-in-Rock as a safe haven. But they were not there long before they wore out their welcome. A boat had been lured ashore and all but one crew member killed. The Harpes took the survivor, tied him on a blindfolded horse and stampeded the horse over a 100 foot cliff to the cave below. The brothers thought this was a hilarious prank, but it so unnerved the other criminals that the Harpes were told to move on.

In September 1799 the Harpes were alleged to have sought refuge at the home of a man they knew near Dixon, Kentucky. They had to share a room with a traveling surveyor whose snoring bothered them, so they killed him. Then they killed the man's wife and child and two neighbors who were unfortunate enough to have seen them. After burning the house and stealing the surveyor's horse, they took off just ahead of a posse that included their former friend. It was this man who got close enough to fire a shot that paralyzed Big Harpe. The murderer stayed in the saddle but was unable to spur his horse and was easily captured. Wiley was able to escape the posse.

As he lay dying alongside the road, Big Harpe supposedly confessed to eighteen killings and said the only murder he regretted was of his own child. According to legend, when his former friend started to cut his head off, Big's last words were, "you're a rough butcher, but cut and be damned." He did, and Micajah's head was displayed prominently alongside a road that came to be called Harpe's Head Road.

By this time, Mason had decided to move on. He had a knack for knowing when an operation was about played out, and he knew that soon vigilantes would come to Cave-in-Rock. Also, he knew just how he could expand his business. Mason had begun to steal entire boatloads of cargo, and after disposing of the crews, would have his own men continue the journey, sell the cargo, and return with the profits. However, not all partners returned promptly, so Mason decided to move downstream and become more directly involved at the source of the cash. He now began robbing travelers who were returning north by way of the Natchez Trace.

But first he shrewdly applied for a Spanish passport. In the spring of 1800, the Spanish controlled all land west of the Mississippi as well as the mouth of the river at New Orleans. A passport gave Mason permission to live on the western side, so he could commit his crimes on the American side and then return to the safety of Spanish territory.

Americans returning from selling their cargoes downstream would walk the rough 550 miles from Natchez to Nashville, where they could travel by water on the Cumberland River back to the Ohio. Laden with loot from their sales, these travelers were ripe targets for Mason's gang. The only man safe from their depredations was John Swaney, the mail rider who covered the Trace at this time. Mason, according to Swaney, claimed that money was "all he was after and if he could get it without taking life he would certainly shed no blood." Of course, this gentleman bandit had no qualms if others got involved in murder, as long as his hands were clean.

Swaney also kept Mason informed with what was being said about him in Natchez, so he accorded him safe passage. Swaney gave a description of the seldom-seen Mason, saying "he weighed 200 pounds and was a fine-looking man. He was rather modest and unassuming and had nothing of the raw-head-and-bloody-bones appearance his character would indicate." There was one other distinctive characteristic that Mason had. According to one contemporary, he had "something ferocious in his look, which arose particularly from a tooth which projected forwards, and could only be covered with his lip by effort."

Mason's wife had supposedly left him because of his ways, and lived downstream with her daughter and one son. The other three sons remained part of Mason's gang, along with such killers as a man called John Setton, who looked a lot like Wiley Harpe. Mason's syndicate also had partners working in Natchez. A merchant named Anthony Glass had helped lay out the Natchez Trace, and he served as Mason's fence who sold stolen goods for him.

On one occasion Mason sent his son John to Natchez to trade with Glass and someone recognized him from a previous roadside robbery. Despite hiring the best lawyer the Mason syndicate could get, young Mason was convicted and sentenced to receive 39 lashes. This was another reason the Masons didn't like to leave witnesses.

With their depredations increasing, the ire of officials increased and the Governor of Mississippi Territory complained that "the road from this territory is infested by a daring set of robbers, and among them are a certain Samuel Mason and a certain Wiley Harp." Eventually a $900 reward was offered for the capture of Mason. When Mason saw his poster after a robbery, he read it aloud with great amusement to his less literate gang. This may have been a fatal mistake as it put ideas in the minds of his henchmen.

Things started to unravel for Mason in 1803 when his gang was arrested by Spanish authorities. John Setton immediately agreed to testify against his boss and the whole crew was sent downriver to Spanish headquarters in New Orleans for further questioning. Here it was determined that Mason had committed no crimes against Spanish citizens but there was sufficient evidence to extradite him to the Americans. They were ordered upstream to Natchez to face trial in U.S. territory.

On the way north their boat had to pull in for repairs that involved most of the guard. Mason's men took advantage of this to pull off a daring escape on March 26, 1803, in which the guard commander fired a dying shot that wounded Mason in the head. The gang fled, although they now remained on the American side of the river.

The reward for Mason now rose to $1000—Dead or Alive. This really amounted to a bounty for killing him since there was no incentive to feed a captive who might escape, when the pay was the same for his body. It is said that in July of 1803 a desperado named James May arrived in Natchez and claimed to have killed Mason, but as he offered no proof he was given no reward.

In November of that year May allegedly returned to Natchez with John Setton and a large ball of clay that turned out to be Mason's head wrapped up "to prevent putrefaction." These two partners had made sure that Mason did "meet a reward adequate to his merit" and now they were out to collect their own reward. In the more colorful versions of the story, there was some controversy when Mrs. Mason refused to positively identify the head, but it was believed she wanted to deny the turncoats the reward. Everyone recognized the fanged skull as Mason's and the reward money was approved.

The story goes that $1000 was such a large sum that it was not readily available in the territorial capital. While impatiently waiting for the cash to be sent, Wiley and his stolen horse were recognized by the victim of that crime. He denied being Wiley Harpe, but another witness told of where he had given Wiley a scar in a knife fight, and "John Setton" had the same scar. May and Harpe were arrested and convicted. Like many of their ilk, they were then separated from their heads, which were put on poles and displayed prominently on the Natchez Trace.

Much of this anecdotal material is colorful but unverified. But there are two facts of the story that are certain. On February 8, 1804 James May and John Setton were executed by hanging in Natchez. And nothing was ever heard from Wiley Harpe or Samuel Mason again.

CHAPTER SIX
William Wells
"A disposition for intrigue"

Of the many factions competing for control of the trans-Allegheny region, none fared worse than the original inhabitants. The Native Americans already living here were unable to compete with the more technologically advanced and numerous Europeans who sought their land. They were not even able to help negotiate their fate, as treaties were made along white man's terms and legal concepts alien to them. There were some whites familiar with Indian life who attempted to speak for the Indians, but some of these men were suspect. William Wells, a white who was raised by Indians, is a prime example. Wells betrayed both his adopted and native races in times of war and peace alike, yet he died a hero's death. He remains one of the most controversial figures of the early frontier.

Wells was a native of Pennsylvania, having been born about 1770 just 25 miles south of Pittsburgh. He was the son of Captain Hayden Wells, who served in Dunmore's War and the Continental Army while William was a child. The family also included four older brothers and a sister. In 1779 the family moved down the Ohio to Kentucky, where Captain Wells built Wells' Station thirty miles east of Louisville. William's mother died about this time of an unknown illness, either just before or just after the move. Two years later Captain Wells was killed in a skirmish with Indians under the command of the Mohawk warrior Joseph Brant. His oldest son Samuel was engaged in the same battle.

Samuel Wells also served in some of George Rogers Clark's campaigns and as a soldier was not in a position to raise his orphaned eleven-year-old brother. Custody of William was given to his father's friend Colonel William Pope, who made sure the boy got a basic education. But his education took a different turn in March of 1784 when he was captured by an Indian raiding party while fishing with some friends. The group was swiftly taken across the Ohio and separated.

The fourteen-year-old Wells was taken to a Miami village on Indiana's Eel River, where he was adopted by the family of a chief named Porcupine. Unlike some captives, he thrived in his new environment and embraced Indian life. His adoptive parents approved of the active, freckle-faced, red-haired boy and named him Apekonit, which can be translated as Wild Carrot, or Carrot Top. An intelligent child, he quickly learned the Miami language and way of life.

So thoroughly did the white orphan boy adapt to his new life that he was even allowed to participate in Indian raiding parties. Wells later recalled how he served as a decoy to lure settlers on the Ohio into ambushes with pleas for help. By the time his older white brothers learned of his captivity and contacted him, Wells only barely recalled his oldest brother Samuel. He had a brief visit with white relatives in Louisville but returned to the Miami and resumed fighting against the whites. It is believed that he fought as a young warrior against American commander Josiah Harmar's army in 1790.

This may have been where he came to the attention of Little Turtle, the Miami chief who was just emerging as the chief strategist for the most successful of Indian coalitions. The son of a chief, Little Turtle was born around 1750 and spent his entire life in the area of present-day Fort Wayne, which was unusual for the nomadic Indians. This area was an important point on the Wabash-Maumee portage that connected the Great Lakes to the Mississippi, and the principle Miami town of Kekionga was located here.

Little Turtle first came to prominence as a war chief in 1780 when he led a force that wiped out a party under French Colonel Mottin de la Balme. The Frenchman had come to America with Lafayette and was attempting to lead French traders from Vincennes to attack Detroit. But after they attacked Kekionga and raided stores there, they were surprised in camp by a counterattack, and the entire party captured or killed.

Ten years later, when Harmer led an American army towards Kekionga, Little Turtle abandoned the town. But he lured an American contingent into a carefully planned ambush on October 19 and three days later defeated another group at the town site. These victories raised Indian morale and enhanced Little Turtle's status in a tribal coalition that was emerging to resist the Americans.

The following summer, a mounted militia campaign under James Wilkinson raided the Miami settlements. Among those captured were the Indian wife and child of Wells. Not knowing if they were alive, Wells not long afterwards married Sweet Breeze, the daughter of Little Turtle. Now he was the son-in-law of the Indian's chief tactician, and this bond lasted until both men died within a month of each other.

At this time, General Arthur St. Clair was gathering an army at Cincinnati, and a grand Indian army assembled to contest him. Under the leadership of Little Turtle and Blue Jacket, they resolved to take the battle to the Americans this time. On November 4, 1791 they surprised St. Clair's lumbering, poorly trained army and gave the United States its worst defeat ever. After a heated battle the Americans broke and ran, suffering 913 casualties, including 634 dead, out of 1450 men.

Little Turtle was the tactical architect of this victory, and he gave his new son-in-law a key role. Wells was entrusted with focusing fire on the artillery crews of the ten cannon that the Indians feared. He was so successful in this that only one artillery officer survived the battle, and all ten field pieces were captured and hidden. Wells also participated in the slaughter after the Americans ran, and he later said he was so busy with his tomahawk that day that afterwards he could barely lift his arm above his head.

This was a great victory for the Indians, but it left Wells feeling unsettled. He was free to visit his white relatives and was having misgivings about fighting his native race, especially since his brother had fought on the other side at St. Clair's Defeat. What may have disturbed Wells even more was that he had seen the white world and realized that the Indians had no chance to prevail in the long run.

While in Cincinnati to search for his first wife and daughter, Wells found employment as an interpreter for a treaty making contingent led by U.S. Peace Commissioners Rufus Putnam and John Heckewelder. Traveling to Vincennes in summer of 1792, he also used his hunting skills to keep the expedition supplied with meat. He later rejoined the Miami but by now had decided to cast his lot with the whites. He openly declared this to Little Turtle, who shared Wells' concern about the Indians' future, and the two parted amicably.

Wells was received with suspicion by the Americans, so he sought to prove himself by revealing where the Indians had hid the cannon that they were unable to transport after St. Clair's Defeat. This later helped Fort Recovery, which Wayne built on the battle site, to repel an Indian attack that Wells warned the garrison about. He was then given the task of reporting on a large Indian conference being held at present-day Defiance in the summer of 1793. As someone dressing and speaking like a Miami, Wells was able to attend this conference. In September he returned and gave three days' worth of reports to General Anthony Wayne, the new American commander.

Wayne was naturally reluctant to trust Wells at first, but he had a theory about how to ensure future loyalty. Calling Wells "one of my confidential agents," he wrote, "I have made it in his interest to be and continue faithful to the United States, for this campaign at least." Wayne's secret ingredient was money, as he claimed "for unless the public reward those kind of people with some degree of liberality—they cannot expect to be served with fidelity in the future." Wayne later came to trust Wells implicitly, but his largesse with federal funds gave Wells a taste of wealth that may have harmed American interests in the long run.

As Wayne prepared to do battle with the Indians in 1794, he approached Wells and "appointed him Captain of a small corps of confidential spies." Wells and his men played a key role in balancing the intelligence gap with the Indians. Many of his scouts were also former captives who were stealthy enough to beat the Indians at their own game. They could infiltrate Indian parties and bring captives back for interrogation and locate signs of war parties. And Wells had additional value, because as the son-in-law of the enemy commander, he was a high-placed defector who knew the mindset of their high command.

Wells and his rangers were soon involved in colorful adventures. Their work was clearly dangerous, for when one of Wells' top men was captured, the Indians punished him by tying him to a tree with a target over his heart and using him for shooting practice until his body was riddled with bullets. On one occasion Wells and two scouts saw three Indians and resolved to kill two and take the third to interrogate. They were amazed to find the brave they spared was the brother of one of the scouts who had been taken captive at the same time. Wells' last daring exploit came right before the Battle of Fallen Timbers. He left Fort Defiance with a small group of scouts and soon took a captive. On their return, they ran into a band of warriors and boldly fell in with them and began asking questions to get more information. When the braves became suspicious, Wells and his men had to fight their way out, and Wells was wounded in the wrist and wound up missing the battle.

Little Turtle was at the Battle of Fallen Timbers, but not as commander. He had grown discouraged that every time he defeated the Americans they returned with an even larger army. Now they were led by a general who "never sleeps" and would not allow his army to be surprised. Little Turtle counseled for peace negotiations but was overruled by the war faction, so he turned control over to Blue Jacket and led only his Miami braves in battle. After the Indians were defeated and British support never materialized, Little Turtle's view was vindicated.

After defeating the Indians, Wayne marched upstream and built Fort Wayne near the site of Kekionga. Since a fort had already been erected at the Grand Glaize, the two largest Indian towns now had American forts on them and the Indians had to listen when Wayne proposed treaty negotiations be held at Fort Greene Ville in the summer of 1795. At the Greene Ville Treaty, Little Turtle and Wells were reunited as Wells was named Wayne's chief interpreter. Over 1,100 Indians attended this conference which resulted in the peaceful settlement of Ohio and the ultimate withdrawal of British and Spanish threats to the west. Wayne could basically dictate the terms, but he greatly depended on his twenty-five year old chief translator. The famous painting of the Greene Ville Treaty on display at the Ohio State House depicts this. Many famous people on the scene are portrayed here, such as William Henry Harrison, and both Lewis and Clark. For the Indians, Tarhe of the Wyandots and Blue Jacket of the Shawnee are shown while Little Turtle addresses Anthony Wayne. Standing between his two surrogate father figures is red-haired William Wells in the center of it all.

Little Turtle was the last to sign the treaty but announced he would also be the last to break it. He felt no sense of betrayal at Wells' behavior and even insisted that Wells be put on the federal payroll as an interpreter. Wells now returned to Kekionga and Sweet Breeze, and he resumed a close relationship with his father-in-law. Little Turtle understood white ways and Wells could explain Indian thinking and they were generally in agreement in regards to strategy. Both came to feel that the key to Indian survival was to adopt white methods such as agriculture.

In 1796, several of the Greene Ville chiefs journeyed to Philadelphia to meet with President Washington and Wells accompanied Little Turtle as his translator. It was the first of several trips to the American capital as the two became familiar with the first three U.S. Presidents. Late in 1797, Little Turtle and Wells returned to Philadelphia and spent much of the winter there. They were given a letter of introduction to President John Adams by James Wilkinson, who had succeeded the recently deceased Wayne as military commander. In addition to the president, they also met the Polish patriot Thaddeus Kosciusko, who was visiting there, and Little Turtle was given a smallpox vaccination by Dr. Benjamin Rush, a signer of the Declaration of Independence. Little Turtle also had his portrait done by Gilbert Stuart, the famous artist who painted the first five U.S. Presidents. Unfortunately, this painting was destroyed when the British burned the White House in 1814.

The pair also met French Count Constantin Volney, who was engaged in research on Indians and Indian language. Volney met with Wells a dozen times and compiled a Miami vocabulary with his assistance. In frank discussions with Volney, Wells' chief complaint about the Indians was that they lived "almost wholly to the present" and gave "little or no remembrance to the past, and hope nothing for the future." Concerning their fatalism in the face of a harsh world, Wells said of the Indian warrior "death becomes so familiar to him that he regards it with indifference; when inevitable he resigns himself to it; or braves it with alacrity."

In addition to such cultural work, Wells and Little Turtle were also engaged in earnest lobbying. The Indian culture was warrior-dominated, and they hoped to take them to a newer phase of development. The various tribes had already become addicted to white-introduced improvements such as woven blankets, metal pots and firearms, and the pair hoped to adapt them further to white ways such as agriculture. They showed vision in recognizing this, but had difficulty implementing specific programs.

One thing they wanted eliminated in the future was alcohol, a scourge so deadly that Little Turtle claimed, "we had better be at war with the white people, for the liquor they introduce into our country is to be feared more than the tomahawk." On a third capital visit, this time to see President Jefferson in Washington in 1802, Little Turtle asked for federal control of the liquor trade. He also requested agricultural and metal working instruction and a blacksmith and trading post for his people.

This effort led to the establishment of the factory system for regulating Indian commerce. The government storehouse, or factory, was an effort to control the Indians as well as keep them sober and uncheated. One of the first Indian agencies set up was at Fort Wayne, where John Johnston was named factor, or business manager. The Indian agent, who was responsible for the execution of government policy, was to be William Wells.

As federal Indian agent, Wells walked a tightrope. He reported to both Indiana Territorial Governor William Henry Harrison and Secretary of War Henry Dearborn, whose goals were not always the same. But in addition to following the political policy of the administration, he also was an advocate for the Indians, even though he was not paid by them. Wells certainly deserved a chance to do this job, as he had managed in wartime to kill both whites and Indians without alienating either. But in seven years of peacetime as

Indian agent at Fort Wayne, Wells managed to alienate just about everyone.

Part of the problem was the nature of the job itself. After Fallen Timbers, the Indians realized they had to deal with the Americans on their own, as they could no longer play various nations off of each other. The tribes gradually sold off land and began to grow dependent on annual payments, called annuities, of cash or salt or other valuable goods otherwise unavailable to them. This sort of welfare demeaned the tribes, as Harrison called the Miami a "poor, miserable drunken set, diminishing every year. Becoming too lazy to hunt, they feel the advantages of their annuities."

Harrison was also part of the problem as he aggressively pursued land cessions in a series of coercive treaties that often bought land from tribes that had no clear right to the area in question. Wells opposed this policy, although not necessarily on behalf of all Indians. As early as 1795, he and Little Turtle had gotten all six Miami clans recognized as separate tribes, which gave them six annuity payments while other tribes had to settle for a single payment. While Wells always favored his Miami tribe, he also advised other tribes they were not being dealt with fairly.

Harrison complained that "Captain Wells has certainly not exerted himself to pacify the Indians who have taken offence at the late treaties" and sent Territorial Secretary John Gibson to investigate. Gibson reported that Wells had told the Delaware tribe their payment was a "mere trifle" and that they had been cheated. Although Harrison claimed "Nine-tenths of the tribe... utterly abhor Wells and the Turtle," he knew he needed their influence on his side and he patched up his differences with Wells at Vincennes in 1805.

Wells also had his hands full with the factor John Johnston, who accused him of corruption. Johnston had been a wagoneer for Anthony Wayne and involved in the mercantile business before his federal appointment. He was a serious, pious man intent on bettering the Indians' lot, and through a career that lasted until 1830 the Indians often requested to deal with him. He even managed to get whites convicted of murdering Indians, which was almost unheard of on the frontier. Charles Dickens met Johnston in 1843 and described him as a "mild old gentleman." But Johnston's mildness had its limits, as he completely detested William Wells. He called him "too unprincipled to be employed anywhere" and claimed "I could detail to you a thousand instances of his total disregard of everything that is held sacred by honest and honorable men."

Johnston accosted Wells' integrity, claiming, "he has amassed a fortune which is said to be equal to $50,000, and a great proportion of this was derived from the advantages which the public situation afforded." He also complained of Wells' interference in policy, saying, "I am much embarrassed in my proceedings with the Indians by the underhand, insidious, ingenious conduct of Wells who... is adding all in his power to render the Indians discontented with us." Johnston's harsh assessment did not extend to Little Turtle, who he felt was "the superior to Tecumseh in all the essential qualities of a great man," but of Wells he believed, "There does not exist a worse man."

These suspicions of corruption were shared by others, as Dearborn believed that "Wells is too attentive to pecuniary considerations." Harrison added that "he makes more money than any man in the territory—how he can do this honestly I am at a loss to know." Yet the only charge that stuck to Wells was when he was caught taking government fence rails to his own farm. Wells countered that while the government had built a home for Johnston, he was living in a cabin he built himself that was "rotting down over my head." When Wells died, his estate included 320 acres, nine slaves, and over $5,000, which was nowhere near what Johnston claimed but still fairly substantial for someone whose top salary was $750 per year.

Wells also became embroiled in controversy in the efforts to teach agricultural practices to the Indians. The government hired a Quaker named William Kirk to administer this program. Wells objected to Kirk's efforts at least in part because Kirk located his program too far from Little Turtle's village. Kirk also had problems with the language and accounting for his expenses and his program failed. Johnston, whose wife was a Quaker, blamed Wells' interference for the failure. When Kirk also blamed him, Wells was not above threatening the Quaker, saying, "If I find you have actually thrown out a single insinuation that I was the cause of the Indians' rejecting you... I shall consider what present reports say to be true and govern myself accordingly." Kirk later moved on to work with the Shawnee in Ohio, where he had more success.

The warlike Indian braves dismissed farming as women's work, so there was considerable resistance to this effort. This was typified by the Shawnee leader Tecumseh who felt that rather than try to copy white culture, the various tribes should resist white encroachment by unifying and not selling any more Indian land without the agreement of all tribes. Tecumseh represented the political arm of this movement, while his brother The Prophet offered spiritual underpinnings. The Prophet claimed to be a holy man whose visions of unity stipulated a rejection of the entire white culture to ensure a return to Indian days of glory.

The Indians were susceptible to religious revivals such as these and the brothers soon had quite a following. In 1805 they moved their village to present-day Greenville, Ohio and openly welcomed all pilgrims. The village was located just inside the white side of the Greene Ville Treaty settlement line, which alarmed nearby white settlers.

Wells believed that it was "absolutely necessary" the village be moved and he bombarded Dearborn with letters to that effect, even offering personally to lead such a mission. In 1807, Wells took it upon himself to write directly to Tecumseh and demand that they move "in the name of the Great Chief of the United States." Wells demanded a written reply within ten days, but Tecumseh responded that "if he has anything to communicate to me, he must come here." Wells then forwarded a vague reply from Dearborn, which he claimed justified his position, which provoked an angry response from Tecumseh. He retorted, "if my great father, the President of the seventeen fires, has anything to say to me, he must send a man of note as his messenger. I will hold no more intercourse with Captain Wells."

Meanwhile, Ohioans were growing more alarmed, especially after a local settler was killed and scalped. At meetings with whites at Urbana and Springfield, Tecumseh sought to soothe fears, and the personable leader also competed with locals in sporting events and even reminisced with his former foe Simon Kenton. But Ohio Governor Thomas Kirker was still concerned, and in addition to calling out the militia he also sent future governors Thomas

Worthington and Duncan MacArthur to Greenville to investigate.

At this point Tecumseh agreed to go to the state capitol at Chillicothe to reassure all of his peaceful intentions. On September 19, 1807 he completely won over the crowd with a speech that the local paper said was "cool, dispassionate, and rational" made by a chief with "manly, firm, and majestic deportment." The only time Tecumseh grew agitated was on the subject of William Wells, when he said, "Congress has a great many good men. Let them take away Wells and put one of them there. We hate him. If they will not remove him, we will! ...From beginning to end his talk is blackguard. He treats us like dogs." Tecumseh later retreated somewhat and said they would "remove" Wells by bypassing and ignoring him, Although the threat was now calmed, the brothers within the next year relocated their village to the Tippecanoe River in Indiana.

By now Wells had incurred the wrath of Indians and whites alike. Blue Jacket, who was now a supporter of Tecumseh, simply called Wells "a bad man." The Shawnee chief Black Hoof, who encouraged Kirk to teach farming to his people, was angry at the entire Miami tribe and claimed, "We will not have anything to do with them and Mr. Wells in particular." Showing how Wells' credibility was strained with everyone, he was now directed by the War Department to submit all fiscal accounts through Johnston. Dearborn wrote to Johnston of Wells that, "I have lost much of my confidence in his integrity." To Wells he delivered an even stronger rebuke, telling him, "Either you possess no useful influence with the chiefs in your agency or you make an improper use of what you possess. In either case you cannot be considered as well qualified for the place you hold."

Late in 1808, Wells took a delegation of chiefs to Washington and also tried to lobby for continuation of his job. But when a Delaware chief complained to Dearborn about Wells' conduct, the Secretary of War resolved to fire his agent. Wells had gone on to visit relatives in Louisville and was not informed of this decision until he returned to Fort Wayne in April, 1809. Wells did not have far to go when he returned home after his dismissal. He had a 320-acre farm just a mile from the agency along a tributary that had been named Spy Run in his honor.

The lyrically named Sweet Breeze had died in 1805, but Wells retained a close attachment to Little Turtle and the Miami. Wells soon remarried to a white woman from a prominent Kentucky family, and in his brief life he was known to have fathered at least nine children by at least four women. But the four children from his liaison with Sweet Breeze were his strongest attachment. These children were sent to Louisville to be educated after Sweet Breeze died. Of the three daughters, one married a doctor, one a judge, and one a military officer. His son, William Wayne Wells, whose middle name was a tribute to Anthony Wayne, went on to graduate from West Point.

Wells remained in a symbiotic relationship with Little Turtle until the two died in 1812. Little Turtle was now bothered by gout, a white man's disease that had afflicted his rivals, St. Clair and Wayne. But he remained mentally active and enjoyed elder statesmen status both with his own tribe and the government. Johnston felt that Wells led Little Turtle astray, but their relationship may have been more mutual. A British colonel who met Little Turtle in 1794 called him "the most decent, modest sensible Indian I ever conversed with." But since after 1795 Wells was virtually the sole conduit by which Little Turtle communicated with the literate world, it's impossible to determine just what Little Turtle really thought. But there is little doubt their loyalties to their tribe were stronger than to the entire Indian movement.

Now that he was out of power, Wells could speak more freely than ever at the agency, and Harrison soon realized that "if he is not employed and remains where he is, every measure of the government will be opposed and thwarted by himself and the Turtle." Administration officials now decided they could keep a tighter reign on Wells if they had him on their payroll. Harrison approved of this, praising Wells' "knowledge... zeal and industry" while acknowledging that "with them, however, were unfortunately blended a disposition for intrigue and for the accumulation of property."

Johnston strongly disagreed, saying that Wells "defrauded both the Indians and the United States" and he feared "the government saddling the poor Indians with Wells again." It was true that the bulk of complaints against Wells came from just three men—Johnston, Harrison and Dearborn. But these were the three men who worked closest with him. Nonetheless, Wells was rehired in January of 1810, with the Secretary of War telling Harrison he was to be "under your immediate control... where there will be the least necessity of entrusting him with the disbursement of public money."

On reason Wells was needed was that events had proven him correct about the threat presented by Tecumseh and the Prophet. Tecumseh had enjoyed great success in aligning tribes and traveled all over the country to promote the idea of common Indian land ownership. When Harrison negotiated a large land purchase at the Treaty of Fort Wayne in 1809, Tecumseh openly threatened chiefs who had agreed to sell. At a conference in Vincennes the next year, Tecumseh and Harrison nearly came to blows discussing the issue. Wells, who was as good at ferreting out information as he was at spreading misinformation, could be useful in such tumultuous times.

Tecumseh was rumored to be in alliance with the British, but, like Little Turtle, he distrusted them and felt they used Indians as cannon fodder. However, Harrison became so sufficiently alarmed that he got federal approval for pre-emptive action. He waited until autumn of 1811, when he knew Tecumseh was in the south recruiting new alliances, before marching on Tippecanoe. The Prophet had been told not to engage the whites in battle, but after convincing his braves they would not be harmed, he authorized an attack. The Americans, whose militia leaders included Wells' brother and new father-in-law, held off the assault and destroyed Prophetstown.

This drove Tecumseh firmly into the British camp by the time war with England was declared on June 18, 1812, ending seventeen years of peace on the frontier. Harrison now saw a definite need for Wells, saying "hated and feared as he is by a great majority of the surrounding Indians, he is nonetheless able, from his influence over a few chiefs of great ability, to effect more than any other person." But this changed on July 14 when the 62-year-old Little Turtle died in Wells' home. He was given a grand funeral at the agency, and was irreplaceable in terms of influence.

The war began badly for the United States. An army under Michigan Territorial Governor William Hull had briefly invaded Canada, but soon was holed up in Detroit thanks to aggressive maneuvers by Tecumseh and the

British. And the disorganized Americans communicated so poorly that the commander at Fort Michilimackinac did not even know he was at war until he was surrounded by British troops demanding his surrender.

The fall of this fort put Fort Dearborn at present-day Chicago at risk, as both land and water supply routes were unsafe. An increasingly nervous Hull ordered Captain Nathan Heald to destroy all stores and abandon Fort Dearborn. This order came by way of Fort Wayne, where Wells was asked to help facilitate the evacuation, and he left along with a retinue of about thirty Miami braves.

Wells had a personal interest in the safety of the garrison, as Heald was his nephew, having married Samuel Wells' daughter. He also knew Indians were eager to be on the winning side. A large number of Indians had already gathered outside the fort and were well aware of recent American setbacks. The garrison might be safe inside the fort, but was extremely vulnerable on a journey to Fort Wayne through Indian-infested country. Wells arrived at Fort Dearborn on August 13 and tried to convince Heald to hold the fort. But Heald insisted on obeying orders and ordered the fort's provisions distributed to Indians he felt to be friendly. He did destroy all extra ammunition and liquor supplies, which were the items most desired by the Indians outside the gates.

For years Wells had carefully chosen sides based on the likely winner, yet now he was faced with dying in a hopeless fight. He had spent his peacetime years engaged in schemes and profiteering the white man's way. Now that he was at war again, he remembered his Indian upbringing. He had told Count Volney that when faced with death, the Indian "braves it with alacrity," and he consciously set out to die that way. Painting his face black, an Indian sign of impending death, he led the garrison out of the fort on the morning of August 15, 1812.

The Americans, who numbered fewer than 100 including their families, had gone only a few miles before they were attacked by over 400 warriors. Wells fought fiercely and bravely in a doomed cause, killing seven men personally before falling. The entire force was either killed or captured and the treatment of Wells' body indicates both the hatred and respect the Indians had for him. His head was cut off and displayed as a sign of contempt, but his heart was cut out and eaten by braves who admired his courage and wanted a part of his heart in them.

The day after the Dearborn Massacre, Hull surrendered Detroit without firing a shot. Two weeks later, Fort Wayne was surrounded and the factory burned, although the only man killed was Johnston's brother. The siege was lifted by soldiers under Harrison, who had resigned his governorship to take command of the army. In the next year, Harrison reversed these initial losses and was able to recapture Detroit and invade Canada, where he defeated the British and Indians in a battle where Tecumseh was killed.

After this conflict, never again would foreign powers threaten the American heartland. And never again would Indians be in any position to resist white encroachment in the region. And there would never be another figure like William Wells straddling relations between Indians and whites.

CHAPTER SEVEN

The Burr Conspirators

"The most finished scoundrel that ever lived"

After defeating both the British and Indians, the new American nation should have been able to maintain control of the land beyond the Appalachian Mountains. Yet there were still internal and external problems that threatened to separate the region from the rest of the country. There were several plotters seeking alliances with foreign powers for establishment of a new nation or vassal state. The most famous plot was the Burr Conspiracy, a colorful and controversial collection of intriguers. While no one was convicted in the circus trial that followed the exposure of this plot, the affair ruined the careers of all connected, with the notable exception of James Wilkinson, who turned in all his partners. Yet Wilkinson, who historian Frederick Jackson Turner has called "the most accomplished artist in treason this country has ever possessed," was the most guilty of all.

There was a geographical reason why land west of the mountains was ripe for intrigue. Every drop of rain that fell from parts of New York to Montana flowed to New Orleans, which had been under Spanish control since 1763. With no roads across the mountains, the only realistic option for shipping goods was down the Ohio and Mississippi rivers, but the Spanish were free to close New Orleans to American shipping.

Spain was worried about the increasing number of American settlers crossing the mountains and was especially fearful their democratic fervor might spread to Spain's vast Latin American colonies. The Spanish hoped to keep the Americans of the western waters in check in part by forming alliances with them that they might separate them or otherwise weaken the union of American states. In addition the British in Canada sought control of western lands at the expense of both the United States and Spain.

To complicate matters further, many westerners felt that the eastern states cared little about solving their shipping problems, and in fact preferred that westerners be forced to send their goods overland to them. In such a climate it was not surprising that many westerners advocated separation from the United States, and used similar arguments that the colonies had used to separate from England.

Some of the more active proponents of such ideas sought alliances with foreign powers. In 1797, William Blount of Tennessee was expelled from the U.S. Senate for actively enlisting British aid for an attack on New Orleans. And Revolutionary War hero George Rogers Clark accepted a major general's commission in the French Army with the same goal in mind. Clark was foiled in part by the efforts of James Wilkinson, which is not surprising because the people betrayed by Wilkinson are a virtual who's who of the founding fathers.

Wilkinson was born in tidewater Maryland in 1757. The son of a planter, he was tutored by a relative who regaled him in with tales of service in the French and Indian War. At the age of sixteen, he was sent to Philadelphia to study medicine. On the first day in town he was fascinated by the military pomp of British soldiers performing drills.

By 1775 he had completed studies and begun practicing in Maryland when the outbreak of the American Revolution revived his dreams of military glory. He eagerly enlisted in the Continental Army as a medical officer and soon found himself in both infantry and staff positions. His first active campaign role was on an invasion of Canada where among his fellow officers were Benedict Arnold and Aaron Burr. All served loyally on this campaign.

Wilkinson in 1777 became a staff aide to General Horatio Gates, the commander of the Northern Department. Gates, a former British officer, was particularly susceptible to flattery, and Wilkinson was adept at offering it to anyone who might be able to advance his career. Wilkinson was promoted and given increased status to where he played a prominent role in the Saratoga campaign. After the British were defeated, it was Wilkinson who helped negotiate much of the surrender terms and introduced the two opposing generals to each other.

Just a few years after marveling at British drill teams he was now supervising the surrender of a 7,000 man British army. Better yet, he was entrusted to personally deliver the glorious news to Congress. And best of all, among the dispatches he carried was a request that the twenty-year-old Wilkinson be promoted to the rank of general.

Wilkinson also enjoyed the prestige and trappings of military travel, and consequently he rarely hurried to end it. It took him eleven days to cover the 285 miles to a waiting Congress, which caused one congressman to remark that his reward should be a pair of spurs rather than a promotion. Wilkinson stopped en route to visit a girl he was courting and also spent a night getting drunk with staff officers of another general.

But Congress could hardly deny Gates any favors, and Wilkinson became a general despite the resentment it caused with more experienced officers. But the new general almost immediately became embroiled in the Conway Cabal, an effort by General Thomas Conway to replace George Washington with Gates. When drinking with officers on his way to Congress, Wilkinson had repeated quotes Conway wrote to Gates and now word got back to Washington and the plot was exposed.

Washington confronted Gates, who denied everything. Gates, with Wilkinson's help, tried to accuse Washington's aide, Alexander Hamilton, with snooping and planting rumors, whereupon Washington told Gates with concealed glee that his source of information was Wilkinson. When Wilkinson was publicly upbraided by Gates, he challenged him to a duel, despite the fact that Gates was not only 30 years older, but also his commanding officer. Washington, who acknowledged Wilkinson was "pompous and ambitious," nonetheless believed that Wilkinson had betrayed the plot out of loyalty to him.

Wilkinson managed to stay out of harm's way for the rest of the war by becoming the army's clothier general, which gave him opportunity to learn about military graft and corruption. He resigned from the army in 1781, after an investigation found "gross irregularities in his accounts." He had married the girl he visited after Saratoga; she was Ann Biddle, a member of a prominent Philadelphia family. And despite whatever other vices he eagerly embraced, he was loyal to his well-connected wife.

After a brief foray into Pennsylvania politics, Wilkinson moved his family to Kentucky in 1784. Here he soon became involved with the issue of western shipping, attending several conferences to discuss political alternatives. Though only twenty-seven, he was already overweight and known for being pompous and humorless. However, he was garrulous, gregarious and generous, and made a good impression with his new neighbors. And while other Kentuckians debated the merits of independence, statehood, or becoming a Spanish colony, Wilkinson swung into action.

In 1787, he traveled down the Mississippi with a cargo of products. He was risking arrest and confiscation of his goods, but he had written ahead to request a meeting with Spanish authorities, who were intrigued by the well-spoken former general. The result of this trip was on August 22, Wilkinson wrote a lengthy memorial, where he announced to Spain he was "transferring my allegiance from the United States to his Catholic Majesty." Wilkinson promised to work for Kentucky separation and to advise Spain on how to deal with the United States. His advice was usually a combination of what the Spanish wanted to hear and what would benefit Wilkinson the most. In exchange for this, Wilkinson requested a generous pension and sole right to ship his goods duty free through New Orleans.

Wilkinson's status was greatly enhanced when he returned to Kentucky in a grand carriage drawn by four horses. He soon had a mansion built on Wilkinson Street in Frankfort, and began to lobby for Kentucky independence. He also sought to serve Spain and himself by starting a rumor campaign that his chief rival George Rogers Clark had become a hopeless drunk.

But Wilkinson was better at intrigue than business and his lavish lifestyle left him overextended by 1791. He also failed to keep Kentucky from becoming a state. But he soon found another opportunity for advancement from the other threat facing Kentuckians—British-sponsored Indian raids on settlements in Kentucky and Ohio. With the U.S. Army's failure to curb this threat, Wilkinson in August 1791 led a mounted militia raid from Cincinnati into present-day Indiana. That fall he was offered a colonel's commission in the regular army, and he resumed his military career.

Wilkinson's previous relations with Spain as a private citizen were merely disreputable. But now as a high-ranking officer in the army, his behavior entered the treasonable as he requested a raise from the Spanish, claiming he could be even more valuable to them now. He also requested that the Spanish not use his name in correspondence, but refer to him as Number Thirteen. Soon after Wilkinson was offered his commission, the Americans suffered a major defeat by the Indians. In the reorganization that followed, Wilkinson was promoted to general, and given responsibility for all frontier forts while overall commander Anthony Wayne recruited and trained a new army in Pittsburgh.

As the ranking officer on the frontier, Wilkinson settled at Fort Washington in Cincinnati, where he had a mansion built and introduced the first carriage to the town. He also had Fort St. Clair built in present-day Eaton, and stipulated that an ornate house also be built there for his use. He continued to accept Spanish largesse, with payments often sent north hidden in barrels. Once his agent was robbed and killed by his guides, but Wilkinson was able to get custody of the killers and hustle them out of the territory before they could blow his cover. Between 1790 and 1794, Wilkinson was paid $32,000 in Spanish gold and silver, more than ten times what he earned as an American general.

Wilkinson's days as an independent operator ended in 1793 when Wayne arrived in Ohio and proceeded to ignore Wilkinson's advice and do things his own way. Wilkinson moved to Fort Hamilton, where he'd had a nice home built for himself and his family, and from there he intrigued against Wayne. So strong was his hatred for his commander that he called him "a liar, a drunkard, a fool… my rancorous enemy, a coward, hypocrite, and the contempt of every man of sense and virtue."

Though able to polarize the officer corps by planting seeds of discord, Wilkinson was unable to prevent Wayne from defeating the Indians and opening the west up for safe settlement. He still complained about Wayne and before leaving for Philadelphia to lodge formal charges, he wrote his Spanish paymasters that the purpose of his trip was "to keep down the military establishment, to disgrace my commander, and secure myself command of the army." These efforts failed, but when Wayne died suddenly in December of 1796, Spanish Agent Number Thirteen became commander of the United States Army.

A treaty with Spain made possible by Wayne's victory had opened the Mississippi for shipping, and as settlement increased in the southwest, Wilkinson spent more time in that area. Spain then fell under the control of Napoleon and the French, who sold New Orleans and much of the entire Mississippi watershed to the United States in 1803. At the transfer ceremony, Wilkinson represented the United States in just the kind of pageantry he delighted in.

The Louisiana Purchase meant that western lands were to play an even bigger part in American politics. This was not lost on Vice President Aaron Burr, who needed to rebuild his political fortunes just about then. Burr came from a distinguished background. His father had been president at Princeton College, and his maternal grandfather was the famous minister Jonathan Edwards. Burr had graduated from Princeton at sixteen and joined the army at the outbreak of the Revolution.

He served briefly as an aide to General Washington but had a personality conflict and preferred a return to the front lines. Here he served with distinction and rose to the rank of colonel while still in his early twenties. After the war, he began a successful law practice in New York City and entered politics. In 1791 he defeated Alexander Hamilton's father-in-law and was elected to the U.S. Senate when he had just obtained the age of 35 that fulfilled Constitutional eligibility requirements. A balding, slight man who stood only about five foot six, Burr nonetheless had a suave, graceful demeanor and dark sparkling eyes and such a persuasive personality that a political opponent admitted Burr "has an address not resistible by common clay." This effect was said to have been even more pronounced among women.

Burr aligned himself with the Jeffersonian party in Congress and while a senator it was he who introduced his former Princeton classmate James Madison to Madison's future wife Dolley. Burr was a vice presidential nominee in 1796. He again filled that slot in the election 1800, as the Jeffersonians needed the New Yorker to geographically balance the ticket. Through a quirk that was soon corrected by the 12th Amendment, there was no distinction between electoral votes for president and vice president. So when Jefferson and Burr tied with 73 electoral votes, the election was thrown to the House of Representatives. Each state delegation had one vote, but in thirty-five ballots taken over five days, neither candidate got the majority of delegations. Burr made no obvious move to usurp authority, but many Jefferson followers felt he was not active enough in yielding. A deal was finally made that enabled Jefferson to take office, but there remained a residue of distrust that pervaded the administration.

In March of 1801, Burr became Vice President of the United States at the relatively young age of 45. Since both men previously elected vice president had gone on to the presidency, there was little reason to doubt that Burr would succeed Jefferson as president. But by the time Jefferson left the White House, Burr had been indicted for murder and treason and had fled the country to avoid trial in Ohio.

His sudden downfall began in 1804 when he decided not to pursue a second term as Vice President. His alienation from the Jefferson faction convinced him a better path to the White House consisted of first solidifying his base. To do this, he ran for Governor of New York in the spring of 1804. However, he was defeated, in large part due to the efforts of his rival, Alexander Hamilton. This left him a lame duck vice president with a questionable future.

A month after his defeat, Burr entertained Wilkinson at Richmond Hill, his New York estate overlooking the Hudson. The two had known each other since 1775, and Burr had previously helped Wilkinson's sons get into Princeton. But on this visit, which Wilkinson made sure took place after dark so he would not be seen, their relationship took a new turn. The partnership formed that evening most certainly had to do with the west, but the specifics remain unknown. The most benign scenario was to start a western colony that would take advantage of a declared war with Spain, while the most extreme theory involved the overthrow of the

United States government. The generally accepted notion was a plan to invade Mexico and separate the western states from the United States.

If Burr felt he needed a fresh political start in the west, this was emphatically confirmed six weeks later when he shot and killed Hamilton in a duel. After an exchange of notes failed to resolve their conflicts, they rowed across the Hudson to New Jersey for their fatal and famous duel. In the history of American scandals, there has never been anything like when the nation's vice president killed the head of the opposition party. In the uproar that followed, Burr was indicted for murder in New Jersey and in New York for violating anti-dueling laws. Though the charges were eventually dropped, Burr fled to Philadelphia, where he stayed with Charles Biddle, a cousin of Wilkinson's wife. Later he went to St. Simons Island off the Georgia coast and stayed at the plantation of a former senate colleague.

He returned to Washington that fall when Congress was in session-- the only time a man under indictment for murder has presided over the United States Senate. Burr was still needed by the administration, as he was to preside over a Senate impeachment trial of a Supreme Court justice that Jefferson hoped to remove. This meant that Burr could still ask favors of Jefferson, and he used this opportunity to get Wilkinson named Governor of the Upper Louisiana Territory headquartered at St. Louis. He also got his brother-in-law named Territorial Secretary and obtained a judgeship in New Orleans for his stepson.

Wilkinson was in Washington at this time, and he and Burr conferred frequently and pored over maps of the western country. Burr also met with the British ambassador to request funding and naval support for an effort to seize

New Orleans and launch an attack on Britain's enemy Spain. Burr fulfilled the last of his duties and was out of a job when Jefferson's second term began in March of 1805.

However, the observant French ambassador had noticed that plans were afoot, and he observed, "Mr. Burr's career is generally looked upon as finished; but he is far from sharing that opinion, and I believe he would rather sacrifice the interests of his country than renounce celebrity and fortune... Louisiana is therefore to become the theatre of Mr. Burr's new intrigue; he is going there under the aegis of General Wilkinson." Concerning Wilkinson, the ambassador has this to say: "Though said to be well informed on civil and political matters, his military capacity is small. Ambitious and easily dazzled, fond of show and appearances, he complains rather indiscreetly, and especially after dinner, of the forms of his government."

Burr's first step as a private citizen was to announce the formation of a company that planned to build a canal around the Falls of the Ohio at Louisville. This gave him the opportunity to set up a bank and borrow money for his real purpose. His partners in this venture were Senator John Smith of Ohio, and Jonathan Dayton, a retiring New Jersey senator, former Speaker of the House, and land speculator for whom the Ohio city of Dayton is named. Burr now planned a western trip, taking care to stay away from legal troubles in New York and New Jersey.

Late in April he left Pittsburgh, floating down the Ohio in a luxurious boat that had cost $135 to equip with such amenities as glass windows and a fireplace. He found he was welcome everywhere, as the westerners had no qualms about dueling and had not been supporters of Hamilton. Early in May, he arrived at Marietta, where he was told of a man who had built a mansion on an island in the Ohio just fourteen miles downstream. He offered to deliver a microscope that the owner had ordered from the east in exchange for a letter of introduction, and on May 5, Burr landed on Blennerhassett Island.

Harman and Margaret Blennerhassett were a wealthy Irish couple who had migrated to the American frontier. Harman was born in 1764, the youngest child of a family that owned a stone mansion on a 7,000 acre estate called Castle Conway. English law of primogeniture stipulated that the oldest son inherit all family holdings, so younger sons were educated to a profession, while for daughters the only career option available was to marry well. Harman was sent to Dublin's prestigious Trinity College, and he also went to law school in that city.

He never had to practice, as the deaths of his older brothers and their father left him the heir to Castle Conway in 1792. He might have lived out his days as an obscure country gentleman had he not courted controversy in two ways. In college, he had become enamored of the spirit of the French Revolution, and he now joined the Society of United Irishmen, an outlawed radical group dedicated to evicting the English from Ireland. Then, in 1794, he married Margaret Agnew, a lovely twenty-three-year old woman, but who happened to be his sister's daughter.

This incestuous union was enough of a scandal that the couple resolved to move as far away as possible. Harman sold Castle Conway for $140,000 and with this huge sum they came to America. They did not locate on the eastern seaboard as they feared discovery of their secret, which remained undisclosed until 1901. Their romantic notions of the new frontier led them west and the winter of 1797 found them in Marietta. Here they found a community to their liking and they purchased part of an Ohio River island located between Belpre and Parkersburg. Their theoretical love of liberty did not prevent them from owning slaves, and islands in the Ohio were considered a part of Virginia, which was a slave state.

It took two-and-a-half years to have their showcase mansion built on this island. The Blennerhassetts spared no expense, as they even shipped 36 panes of glass across the roadless mountains, with the result that their home had more glass windows than the new Ohio capitol building in Chillicothe. The home cost $40,000 to build, and their influx of hard cash did much to keep the local economy afloat. When the mansion and its luxurious gardens were complete, they were a marvel to all river travelers. In contemporary descriptions, the phrases "terrestrial paradise" and "enchanted island" were repeated often.

But their eagerness to spend lavishly had a downside, as the locals discovered that Blennerhassett's wealth was exceeded only by his gullibility. He became the target of all sorts of schemes, and through this, extravagant spending, and poor business sense, he started rapidly going through his supposedly limitless fortune.

Harman was also the butt of some local humor. Tall and thin with a stooped posture, he also had what was called "dancing eye," a condition where his pupils seemed to dart about. This may have been connected to his extreme nearsightedness that was also a source for jibes. While Blennerhassett had a large library, performed scientific experiments and supported local music, this ineffectual intellectual's reputation, according to his business partner, was that he had "every kind of sense but common sense."

Margaret Blennerhassett fared better in the estimation of her neighbors. She was as cultured as her husband, speaking French fluently as well as composing poetry. But the tall, attractive woman was also an excellent horsewoman known for riding at a breakneck pace between Belpre and Marietta. She was a gracious hostess at balls at the mansion, and so civic-minded that when she obtained smallpox vaccine for her children she also arranged for many local children to be vaccinated.

When Burr came to call on this couple, both parties were surprised at the cultured demeanor of the other. In a long evening of lively conversation there were few specifics of Burr's venture discussed. But the seeds were planted and in the correspondence that followed, Burr was able to recruit Blennerhassett and secure a reputation as the serpent in this Eden.

After leaving Blennerhassett Island, Burr proceeded west and was welcomed at every stop. He visited numerous frontier leaders and stopped at many manors that had names. Among the estates he stayed at were: Ohio Senator Thomas Worthington's Adena at Chillicothe, Indiana Territorial Governor William Henry Harrison's Grouseland at Vincennes, and Andrew Jackson's Hermitage at Nashville. To each host he told about as much of his plans as he felt they wanted to hear. To Blennerhassett he spoke of a vast empire with Harman returning home in triumph as Ambassador to Great Britain. To the more patriotic Jackson he mentioned only invading Mexico after war with Spain was declared, as Jackson had already advocated that America cut "through the damned greasers to the City of Mexico."

On June 6, Burr caught up with Wilkinson at Fort Massac, near where the Ohio joins the Mississippi.

Wilkinson was en route to his governor's position in St. Louis, but he and Burr remained cloistered for four days of intensive consultation. Wilkinson then provided Burr with use of an ornate military barge to proceed to New Orleans, where he arrived June 25.

This cosmopolitan city was the key to all plans, and a likely capital for any future empire. Founded by the French, it had been under Spanish administration for most of the past forty years, and also featured a number of slaves, free blacks, and Caribbean natives. How this polyglot population would react to a new government under English-speaking Protestants was a source of much speculation.

There were still few Americans in the city, but some interesting ones. One was Irish-born Daniel Clark, an associate of Wilkinson's, who had formed the Mexican Society, which was dedicated to freeing Mexicans from Spanish rule. Another was Edward Livingston, a celebrated lawyer whose wealthy clients ranged from the pirate Jean Lafitte to a corporation trying to corner a monopoly on the infant steamboat trade. He had served in Congress and as mayor of New York City before obligation for a friend's debt had led him to make a fresh start in New Orleans. He later became Jackson's Secretary of State. Livingston's brother Robert had helped negotiate the Louisiana Purchase while serving as Ambassador to France.

Burr saw much and was seen much in New Orleans. He decided he needed someone stationed there to watch his interests and assigned this task to Dr. Erich Bollman. The Burr Conspiracy is so colorful that even the peripheral characters are fascinating. Justus Erich Bollman was born in Hanover, Germany in 1769. He studied medicine, but like many a doctor of that era, he seemed to prefer adventure and intrigue to medicine.

Bollman was living in Paris during the worst of the French Revolution, when either being educated or a foreigner was cause for suspicion. Despite this he was able to smuggle a wanted former government official out of the country to London. Buoyed by this success, he set out to free Lafayette, who had been imprisoned at an unknown location by Austria after defecting from the French Army.

He was able to confirm Lafayette's location by befriending the prison surgeon at a suspected possible location. He arranged for his new friend to deliver open letters to Lafayette – but these letters included post-scripts written in lemon juice, an early form of invisible ink. In this way, the two made plans for an escape to take place during the prisoner's daily carriage ride. To do this, Bollman needed a partner with a second horse. In Vienna, he happened to meet an American named Francis Huger, yet another medical student turned adventurer, who was touring Europe. By a fantastic coincidence, it was at Huger's father's house that Lafayette has spent his first night in America, and Huger pronounced it a point of honor that he be allowed to help rescue Lafayette. The pair did manage to overpower the guard and free Lafayette, but the three foreigners were easily recognized and captured. After eight months imprisonment, Bollman was released and came to America, where he was celebrated as a hero. He wound up in New York, where he was recruited by Burr for his linguistic and espionage skills.

After staying with Livingston for three weeks, Burr returned north via the Natchez Trace, meeting with more people along the way. His activities had aroused suspicion and some accusations of illegal activity had been published.

These reports alarmed Wilkinson, already rumored to be on the Spanish payroll, and he began to withdraw from communications with Burr. He also was busy in St. Louis, where as both military and civil commander and arbiter of all land disputes he practically had a license to print money. He also kept up on his work for the Spanish, keeping them apprised of the Lewis and Clark expedition then in progress, and urging Spain to arrest the pair.

Burr returned to Washington over the winter of 1805-1806 to see how his lobbying efforts there had worked out. The news was bad. The British Ambassador informed him there would be no fiscal or naval support for his venture. And in a courtesy call on Jefferson he ascertained there was unlikely to be a war with Spain, which Burr needed as a pretext to invade Mexico. To address his funding problems, he renewed his correspondence with Blennerhassett, who was rapidly running through his inheritance and eager to finance a project that might restore his fortune.

The following August, Burr returned to Blennerhassett Island. In Marietta, he was feted at a ball and invited to review the militia. While in town he also contracted with Blennerhassett's business partner for construction of fifteen large boats, which were paid for by Blennerhassett. The island was now set up as a gathering point for men and supplies, and became a beehive of activity that aroused the suspicion of neighbors. Burr stayed only briefly before leaving to set up other staging areas at Lexington and Nashville.

Following behind soon afterwards came another secret weapon in the form of Burr's daughter Theodosia. Burr was considered, then as now, to be a cynical, amoral libertine who was a combination of Machiavelli and

Casanova. Yet he was also a devoted husband and father, and one of the nation's first feminists. When he married in 1782, it was to Theodosia Prevost, a widow ten years older who had neither beauty nor wealth. But she was a lively intellectual companion for him, and he did no womanizing until after her death in 1794.

The only surviving child of this union, a daughter named for her mother, became the repository for all of Burr's ideas. When she was still an infant, Burr wrote to her mother that "if I could foresee that Theo would become a mere fashionable woman, with all the frivolity and vacuity of mind… I would honestly pray God to take her forthwith hence. But I yet hope by her to convince the world what neither sex appears to believe—that women have souls."

Burr gave detailed instructions for his daughter's education, and corresponded with her daily while he was away in the senate, correcting her grammar and spelling and stressing foreign languages. Theodosia thrived under this attention, and she was so precocious that at thirteen she hosted a formal dinner party for Indian diplomat Joseph Brant in her father's absence. A slim brunette with soulful brown eyes, she was so intelligent and charming that everyone fell under her spell. That she met her father's high standards was shown when he wrote to her the night before his duel with Hamilton, when he realized he might die the next day, "I am indebted to you, my dearest Theodosia, for a very great portion of the happiness which I have enjoyed in this life. You have completely satisfied all that my heart and affections had hoped or even wished."

In 1801, the seventeen-year-old Theodosia had married Joseph Alston, a South Carolina planter who was one of the wealthiest men in the country. Now this couple came west, along with their only child, Aaron Burr Alston, called Gamp by his doting grandfather. Everyone fell victim to Theodosia's charms, although her husband was less well thought of. Margaret Blennerhassett wrote, "I never could love one of my own sex as I do her," but added, "How can she live with a man such as Alston?"

Alston was underwriting much of Burr's operations, but a series of crop failures had left him with cash flow problems. Blennerhassett had more access to his money and he supplied it with the understanding that Alston would indemnify him against future losses. In addition to supplies and equipment, a major expense was the purchase of a large tract of land in Louisiana. This gave them the pretext of merely being legitimate settlers in case war with Spain did not materialize.

War almost did break out in 1806 when a Spanish force crossed the Sabine River that today divides Texas and Louisiana. The terms of the Louisiana Purchase were very vague about its borders, and armies were required to define the final dimensions. Spanish troops on soil claimed by America could ignite the war that many westerners wanted, and in May, General Wilkinson was ordered to proceed to the Sabine "with as little delay as practicable."

Four months later, Wilkinson was still in St. Louis. He had his reasons, as for one thing his wife was dying of tuberculosis at the time. But he was also understandably reluctant to fight the hand that fed him by starting a war with Spain. Wilkinson currently combined American power with Spanish gold, and he risked losing both by joining Burr. He would be willing to do this if assured of success, but needed time to see how things developed. As pressure mounted, he finally got the push he needed in the form of the now-famous cipher letter.

Wilkinson had finally left St. Louis for Natchez in September, and then took two weeks to travel overland to the Sabine standoff. It was here on October 8 that he was given a letter by Burr's aide Sam Swartwout that was written in a code designed earlier by Wilkinson. The deciphered hieroglyphics revealed a letter from Burr that had been altered, probably by Dayton, as it mentioned Burr in both the first and third person.

The cipher letter was dated July 29 and told Wilkinson: "I have at length obtained funds, and have actually commenced... Wilkinson shall be second to Burr only and Wilkinson shall dictate rank and promotion of his officers. Burr will proceed west 1 August—never to return. With him go his daughter and grandson. The husband will follow in October with a corps of worthies." Dayton had added a letter under his own signature that told Wilkinson, "it is now ascertained that you are to be displaced in the next session... you are not a man to despair or even despond, especially when such prospects offer in another quarter. Are you ready? Are your numerous associates ready? Wealth and glory, Louisiana and Mexico."

Dayton had strengthened Burr's comments and added his letter because he was concerned about Wilkinson's loyalty. By telling him that Jefferson planned on removing him as governor, he hoped to push him off the fence, but it may have pushed him the wrong way. Some feel that Wilkinson planned to betray Burr all along and may even have entrapped him just to turn him in and curry favor with both Spain and the United States. But it is more likely that it was not until he got this letter that he decided to save himself by offering up Burr to both countries. When it came time to choose sides, Wilkinson was on Wilkinson's side, and he served himself well.

Wilkinson now wrote Jefferson that he had uncovered a plot that threatened New Orleans and the nation, and he sent along an altered version of the cipher letter. He also wrote to the Spanish warning them of the plot and unsuccessfully requested a large sum for exposing it. Then, he negotiated a treaty with the Spanish troops opposing him that stipulated both sides retreat until the issue could be negotiated. This freed him to focus on Burr, and for once Wilkinson moved quickly. He returned to Natchez in three days after taking two weeks earlier to cover the same ground. He then proceeded immediately to New Orleans, where he requested the territorial governor declare martial law.

This was denied, but Wilkinson still proceeded to make multiple arrests, especially of people who could do damage to him. Swartwout and Bollman were shipped out of the city in irons and Wilkinson requested they be tried by a military tribunal, which would not be public. An editor who objected was arrested, as was a judge who resigned in protest of Wilkinson's abuses. But it did little good to complain about Wilkinson, as Jefferson, like Washington before him, believed that Wilkinson had revealed the plot out of loyalty to him.

Meanwhile, Burr was floating blithely down the Ohio, unaware that the President was about to call for his arrest. He had been challenged by a grand jury in Kentucky but had not been charged after being represented by Henry Clay, a young lawyer recently elected to the Senate.

Burr also had problems behind him on the Ohio. Rumors and activity on Blennerhassett Island had alarmed neighbors and the Governor of Ohio had called out the militia and on December 9 authorized the seizure of the boats just being completed at Marietta. This sudden confiscation alarmed the recruits who had only recently arrived at Blennerhassett Island, and the conspirators were further alarmed to hear that in Parkersburg the Wood County militia was gathering to come out to the island. They decided to flee and the night of December 10 was a hectic one, as Blennerhassett sold his business interests to his partner and left in the night. The militia arrived at dawn, but by then had little to do but trash the mansion.

Blennerhassett and his crew caught up with Burr at the junction of the Cumberland and Ohio Rivers on December 27. Returning was no longer an option and they proceeded on. When their flotilla arrived at Natchez on January 10, 1807, both the townspeople and Burr were in for a surprise. After hearing terrifying rumors of Burr's army, the citizens now saw that his entire force was less than a hundred men in a handful of boats. As for Burr, he now found out that Wilkinson had betrayed him, and instead of proceeding to the Sabine front, he had to face yet another grand jury.

He was again released, but a judge who was the father of Jefferson's Attorney General ruled that he had to remain in the area. By now Wilkinson had offered a reward for Burr's capture, and Burr feared Wilkinson wanted him dead rather than alive. He skipped bail and tried to go cross-country to Georgia, but was captured in present-day Alabama. Burr was then sent on to Richmond to face a charge of treason.

Richmond was the trial site because Blennerhassett Island, which was alleged to be the key locale of the plot, was a part of Virginia. The presiding judge was to be Chief Justice of the Supreme Court John Marshall, as in those days Supreme Court justices were each assigned to a federal district court as well. Marshall was a distant cousin of Jefferson, but was an avowed political enemy. He did not look too objective right away, as he was seen dining in public in Burr's company during the first week of the hearings. But Jefferson had also tainted the proceedings by announcing that Burr's "guilt was placed beyond question."

In the arraignment phase Marshall had to decide on both treason and misdemeanor charges. The misdemeanor referred to making war on Spain when the United States was at peace, and the treason accusation referred to severing the western states from the union. Marshall approved the misdemeanor count but ruled that a grand jury would have to indict on the treason charge.

Treason is the only crime defined in the Constitution, but Marshall still had to rule on the phrase "levying of war." He decided on a strict definition where actual treason, not just intent, had to have been committed by an armed force. But he did acknowledge that one could importune treason without being physically present. This meant that the prosecution could focus on the activities of December 10 on Blennerhassett Island even though Burr was not there.

The grand jury convened began on May 22 and the event drew spectators from all over the country. Jefferson was about the only one who stayed away, but to monitor the proceedings he sent his protégé, the recently returned explorer Meriwether Lewis. Jefferson also micro-managed the trial from afar, bombarding prosecutor George Hay with some fifty letters. Burr's defense team included such notables as Luther Martin of Maryland, and Edmund

Randolph, who had served as Attorney General and Secretary of State in George Washington's cabinet.

These men knew something about Constitutional law, having served as delegates at the convention that had written the Constitution. Both men ultimately refused to sign the final version, and now both offered their services to Burr for free. Martin was a particularly flashy character, with a booming voice and a jug filled with brandy at his side throughout the trial. It was said he did his best work when he was drunk, and his stamina was not affected, as late in the trial he spoke for fourteen hours straight.

William Eaton, one of the first witnesses called, was just as flamboyant and bibulous as Martin. A former army officer who had impressed Anthony Wayne by learning to speak Miami while at Fort Recovery in Ohio, Eaton later joined the State Department. After doing undercover work during the Blount Conspiracy, Eaton was sent to North Africa as the Consul to Tunis. This was when Barbary pirates were threatening American shipping, and Eaton mastered Arabic and intrigued to replace an anti-American ruler with a more friendly rival. With a motley collection of foreign adventurers on camels, he crossed hundreds of miles of desert and captured the port city of Derne in 1805. This helped end the Tripolitan War on favorable terms, and Eaton returned home a hero. However, he encountered difficulties when he tried to get Congressional reimbursement for his expenses, and his abrasive personality did not help his cause.

A bold adventurer with linguistic ability and a grudge against the administration, Eaton was the perfect recruit for Burr's plans, but Eaton turned him down. And at preliminary hearings, he claimed that Burr planned to loot the New Orleans banks, overthrow the government, and throw

Jefferson into the Potomac. A month after making these claims, his accounts were suddenly resolved in his favor.

Now in Richmond to repeat these charges, he swaggered about town in Arab costume that featured a large hat and Turkish sash. But Marshall's ruling that an overt act had to be proved limited the use of Eaton's testimony. He continued to linger wherever alcohol was served and complain of his treatment. Co-defendant Blennerhassett observed in his diary that "the once redoubted Eaton has dwindled down in the eyes of this sarcastic town into a ridiculous mountebank, strutting about the streets... when he is not tippling in the taverns." Eaton is almost forgotten today, although the Ohio town where Wilkinson built Fort St. Clair is named for him.

The most important witness was Wilkinson, who defense counsel Edmund Randolph called "the alpha and the omega of the present prosecution." Yet Wilkinson was characteristically late to arrive, in part because he had to gather alibis. He convinced the Spanish to ship their archives to Havana, so the governor could honestly state that he had no records in his files that indicated Wilkinson was receiving a Spanish pension. It wasn't until Havana was captured in the Spanish-American War in 1898 that the details of Wilkinson's treason were found, which gave a delayed confirmation to Wilkinson's fear that a declared war with Spain would expose him. Wilkinson's continued absence led to a recess in the proceedings. Washington Irving, who was among the media horde covering the trial, irreverently wrote to a friend that this recess was so the Virginians "might go home, see their wives, get their clothes washed, and flog their negroes."

After resuming in June, Marshall dropped a bombshell when he ruled that Jefferson must supply a copy of the cipher letter. The head of the judicial branch did not require the head of the executive branch to appear in person, so Jefferson complied, although he privately seethed. The same day the prosecution suffered another setback with Bollman on the stand. After being shipped back to Washington, Bollman had a lengthy meeting with Jefferson where he claimed that only Spain was the focus of Burr's plan. He also wrote a lengthy statement that Jefferson promised to keep secret. However, he then shared it with Prosecutor Hay. Now, when Hay offered Bollman a pardon in open court, Bollman angrily refused it, saying acceptance of it would be an admission he had done something wrong.

On June 16, Wilkinson made his long-awaited appearance. In his memoirs, Wilkinson claimed that Burr could not meet his gaze, but Irving wrote that Burr ignored him, save for "one look of withering scorn." Irving described Wilkinson as "strutting and swelling like a turkey cock," and said his testimony was "such a mighty mass of words" that it took "at least two days to discharge the wondrous cargo." Wilkinson proved to be a most unreliable witness, and when he admitted altering the cipher letter to avoid incriminating himself, Hay wrote to Jefferson that "my faith in him is shaken, if not destroyed."

In fact, the grand jury under foreman John Randolph nearly indicted Wilkinson for treason in a close 9-7 vote. Randolph, who was also Speaker of the House of Representatives, had been named foreman by Marshall. A frail, beardless man with a high pitched voice, Randolph may have been shorted on testosterone, but he had an abundance of vitriol that he used on his many political enemies. He particularly detested Wilkinson, who he called "the only man I ever saw who was from the bark to the very core a villain" and "the most finished scoundrel that ever lived." Wilkinson barely escaped indictment, but Burr and Blennerhassett were indicted on both treason and misdemeanor charges on June 24. The same charges soon followed on Dayton, Senator Smith, and three others, although not Bollman or Swartwout.

For the actual trial in August, Theodosia and her family came north to be by Burr's side, which undoubtedly did not hurt his cause. She charmed everyone, particularly Luther Martin, who proclaimed his love so conspicuously that Blennerhassett wrote that Martin's "idolatrous admiration of Mrs. Alston is almost as excessive as my own." Another interested spectator was Andrew Jackson, who felt Wilkinson had entrapped Burr. Jackson said of the defendant, "Burr is as far from a fool as I ever saw, and yet he is as easily fooled as any man I ever knew." As for Wilkinson, Jackson bumped him from a public sidewalk and challenged him to a duel, as did Swartwout, who claimed Wilkinson had stolen his watch. Wilkinson wisely declined these invitations, no doubt aware that Jackson had killed a man in a duel the previous year.

The actual trial was almost anti-climatic, with all efforts focused on one night's events on Blennerhassett Island. It was hard for the government to argue that war was being levied when the "troops", without their leader, had fled the island rather than face a county militia that hadn't even been legally called out. And no doubt it bruised Blennerhassett's ego to be described as having no common sense and unable to tell a man from a horse at ten yards, but it helped his case.

On September 1, the jury deliberated only twenty-five minutes before acquitting Burr of treason. That evening Burr celebrated with a long and public stroll all over town with Theodosia at his side. Two weeks later he also was acquitted on the misdemeanor charge. With the acquittal of the alleged ringleader, all the charges were dropped against all the other defendants, with one exception. Marshall ruled that there was sufficient evidence to pursue the misdemeanor charges against Burr and Blennerhassett in Ohio. Both were ordered to post bail and appear in Chillicothe in January of 1808. This trial was never held, and the charges still stand today.

The Burr trial ruined nearly all the conspirators. Dayton, who had signed the Constitution at 27 and was still only 47, was finished in national politics. Smith, who was among the least culpable, also had his career destroyed. The Senate voted to expel him 19-10, despite the efforts of his defense counsel Francis Scott Key. This was one vote short of the two-thirds majority required, but Smith resigned anyway and returned to Ohio. Here he found the citizens boycotted his mercantile establishment, and he soon left the state and entered obscurity.

The decline of the Blennerhassetts' fortunes was another sad story. They purchased a southern cotton plantation with their dwindling funds, but a series of crop failures left them in even worse shape. They tried to blackmail Alston, but even a partial payment of the $50,000 they claimed he owed them did little to stem their downward slide. Harman was offered a judgeship in Montreal, but it fell through when his benefactor was bitten by a rabid fox and died. The couple finally wound up living with Harman's sister in England, where he died in 1831. Margaret tried to seek redress in the United States and died in New York in 1842. Of their two sons born on the island, one was an alcoholic who disappeared from St. Louis around 1828 and the other a failed artist who died destitute in New York. Even their mansion suffered an unhappy fate, as it was accidentally burned in 1811 by unwelcome intruders of the former island Eden.

The fall was hardest for Burr, and not just because he had farthest to fall. Fearing that the Ohio charges might be pursued, he fled to Europe in 1808, with Theodosia coming north to see him off. He was gone for four years, staying in England with the philosopher Jeremy Bentham and going to Paris in an unsuccessful effort to interest Napoleon in a Mexican scheme. He returned just as the War of 1812 began, which meant the Ohio charges would be forgotten with the nation at war.

But that was the extent of his good fortune, as his first letter after returning home was from a distraught Theodosia saying that Gamp had died of a fever. Burr wrote to Bentham that "Theodosia's boy, her only child, is dead... and I have much reason to apprehend that she will not long survive him." It was decided she should visit her father, but Alston, who had just been elected Governor of South Carolina, stayed behind to help with the war effort. As overland travel was considered too harsh for the suffering Theodosia, she booked passage on the *Patriot*, a ship better known for speed than warfare. On the last day of 1812, Theodosia sailed north along with a trunk of Burr's papers that he had left with her for safekeeping, and which may have contained definitive proof of his guilt or innocence.

The *Patriot* was never heard from again. There were rumors of pirates making all hands walk the plank and there was also a strong storm that battered the coastal waters at the time. But no one really knows for sure what happened to the mystery ship. Joseph Alston's reaction to this tragedy shows that he was not the dull and heartless Philistine his critics felt him to be. Writing to Burr about feeling "severed from the human race," he proclaimed "the man who has been deemed worthy of the heart of Theodosia Burr… will never forget his elevation." Alston's grief proved to be fatal. Three years later, when Burr urged him to challenge the "Virginia Dynasty" of Jefferson, Madison and Monroe that occupied the White House for 24 years, Alston replied, "the energy, the health necessary to give practical effort to sentiment are gone. I feel too much alone, too extremely unconnected to the world, to take much interest in anything." Six months later he was dead at 37, officially of disease but really of a broken heart.

Aaron Burr was too strong to be felled by a broken heart, and he survived another twenty-four years after both his descendants died. He resumed his New York law practice and prospered. Though still considered guilty by many, he was loyal to those who stood by him. When Luther Martin became incapacitated by a stroke, Burr took him into his home and cared for him the last three years of Martin's life. In his 70s, Burr remarried to Madame Jumel, one of the richest widows in New York. Born Betsy Bowen, she had been a prostitute who came to New York and wound up marrying the wine merchant who had kept her as a mistress. Now in her 50s, she wound up suspecting Burr of infidelity and using her money. She petitioned for a divorce that was granted on September 14, 1836, the day Burr died.

Of all the conspirators, the only one to resume a position of prominence was Wilkinson, the one who turned them all in. Though replaced as governor by Meriwether Lewis and no longer used by Spain, he was still returned as commander of the Army. John Randolph pressed for a Congressional inquiry into Wilkinson's Spanish activities, but Jefferson protected his informant and instead ordered a military inquiry by junior officers who quickly exonerated their commanding officer.

Wilkinson returned to New Orleans and immediately became involved in another scandal. He moved the army out of the city to an area that he leased from his future father-in-law at an exorbitant price and then contracted for meat after receiving a kickback. The land proved to be a pestilential hellhole and the meat rancid, and soon Wilkinson's troops were dying like the flies that surrounded them.

When the Secretary of War found out the army was stationed in a swamp below sea level in the tropics under such unsanitary conditions, he ordered Wilkinson to move out in May. Yet Wilkinson did not budge until September, during which time hundreds became sick and died. In addition, Wilkinson's former partner Daniel Clark published a book called *Proofs of the Corruption of General James Wilkinson,* which contained allegations too specific to ignore. Wilkinson was ordered to Washington to face more Congressional investigations and another court martial. His luck held, as his defense counsel was Roger B. Taney, a brilliant young lawyer who would go on to succeed Marshall as Chief Justice. Wilkinson was given another coat of whitewash and returned to command again.

When the War of 1812 began, Wilkinson was promoted to major general. In the thirty-five years since first being made a general, Wilkinson's total battlefield time consisted of about an hour at Wayne's victory at Fallen

Timbers, nearly twenty years earlier. Now, with this promotion, he was expected to lead an independent command into battle, something he had never done. Ordered north in March of 1813, he did not arrive in Washington until July 29, and he tarried there for a month before going to Lake Ontario to plan an invasion of Canada.

Wilkinson's campaign was plagued by his usual squabbles with subordinates and complaints of governmental interference. Though he knew he needed a victory to salvage his reputation, he could not even decide if it was Montreal or Kingston that he wanted to attack, and the season grew late until he finally crossed the St. Lawrence River in October.

Wilkinson was now 56 years old and unused to adverse field conditions, of which an invasion of Canada in November was a prime example. Suffering from numerous physical ailments he took a variety of medications and soon began behaving strangely. He would enthusiastically give complex orders only to gloomily cancel them later. After manic activity he would later curse himself, unusual because Wilkinson normally only cursed others. On the night of November 6, Wilkinson was convivial to the point of giddiness but later he was found staring forlornly into a smoldering campfire. With their commander exhibiting such erratic behavior, the American invasion foundered. Wilkinson was sick in his tent when his troops were defeated by a much smaller British and Canadian force on November 11.

Wilkinson was now discredited for the last time. He was removed from command and ordered to face yet another court martial. When accused of being drunk on the night of November 6, he pointed out that his medicine contained laudanum, the active ingredient in opium. So his defense against a charge of drunkenness was that it was the opium that made him behave so strangely. Wilkinson was still given a final coat of whitewash, but the nation had grown weary of both war and Wilkinson. When the army was downsized at the end of the War of 1812, Wilkinson was dropped from the active rolls.

He now retired to his plantation in New Orleans with his new wife and wrote a three volume book of memoirs. This drew scant attention and not long afterwards he relocated to Mexico City. Here he registered as an agent for the American Bible Association but reportedly was active in lobbying for land grants in Texas. He also allegedly continued his use of opium here. Nothing came of his final schemes and Wilkinson died in Mexico City in 1825.

The failure of Burr's plot ended the last perceived threat to United States control over the heartland. The region, and most westward areas settled afterwards, remained firmly devoted to the American nation. But it should not be forgotten that the area remained American despite a raft of interesting spies, scoundrels and rogues whose efforts might have made it otherwise.

Selected Bibliography

Abernethy, Thomas Perkins. *The Burr Conspiracy*. New York: Oxford University Press, 1954.

Anson, Bert. *The Miami Indians*. Norman, OK: University of Oklahoma Press, 1970.

Banta, R.E. *The Ohio*. New York: Rinehart & Co., 1949.

Burton, Clarence Monroe. *John Connolly: A Tory of the Revolution*. American Antiquarian Society. October 1909: 70-105.

Butterfield, Consul W. *History of the Girtys*. Cincinnati: Robert Clarke & Co., 1890.

Butterfield, Consul W. *Washinton- Irvine Correspondence*. Madison, WI: David Atwood, 1882.

Carter, Harvey Lewis. *The Life and Times of Little Turtle: First Sagamore of the Wabash*. Urbana, IL: University of Illinois Press, 1987.

Chandler, David Leon. *The Jefferson Conspiracies*. New York: William Morrow & Co., 1994.

Connolly, John. *A Narrative of the Transactions, Imprisonment and Sufferings of John Connolly*. London, 1783.

Craig, Neville B, ed. *The Olden Time*. Pittsburgh: Dumars & Co., 1846.

Cuneo, John R. *Robert Rogers of the Rangers*. New York: Richardson and Steirman, 1987.

Hammersmith, Mary Powell. *Hugh McGary, Sr.: Pioneer of Virginia, North Carolina, Kentucky and Indiana*. Wheaton, IL: Nodus Press, 2000.

Hartley, Cecil B. *Lewis Wetzel: The Virginia Ranger*. Philadelphia: G. G. Evans, 1860.

Hill, Leonard U. *John Johnston and the Indians in the Land of the Three Miamis*. Columbus, OH: Stoneman Press, 1957.

Hintzen, William. *The Border Wars of the Upper Ohio Valley 1769-1794*. Manchester, CT: Precision Shooting, Inc., 1999.

Jocobs, James Ripley. *Tarnished Warrior: Major General James Wilkinson*. New York: MacMillan, 1938.

Kellogg, Louise Phelps. *Frontier Advance on the Upper Ohio 1778-1779*. Madison, WI: Wisconsin Historical Society, 1916.

Kellogg, Louise Phelps. *Frontier Retreat on the Upper Ohio 1779-1781*. Madison, WI: Wisconsin Historical Society, 1917.

Lomask, Milton. *Aaron Burr: The Conspiracy and Years of Exile, 1805-1836*. New York: Farrar, Strouss, Giroux, 1982.

Rogers, Robert. *A Concise Account of North America*. New York: Johnson Reprint Corp., 1966.

Rogers, Robert. *Journals of Major Robert Rogers*. Ann Arbor, MI: University of Miami, 1966.

Rosenthal, Baron De (John Rose). *Journal of A Volunteer Expedition to Sandusky from May 24 to June 13, 1782*. Reprinted from the Pennsylvania Magazine of History and Biography, July and Oct., 1894.

Rothbert, Otto A. *The Outlaws of Cave-In-Rock*. Carbondale, IL: Southern Illinois University Press, 1996 reprint.

Sipe, C. Hale. *The First American Frontier: Fort Ligonier and Its Times*. Harrisburg, PA: The Telegraph Press, 1933.

Swick, Ray. *An Island Called Eden*. Parkersburg, WV: Blennerhassett Island Historical State Park, 1996.

Talbert, Charles Gano. *Benjamin Logan: Kentucky Frontiersman*. Lexington, KY: University of Kentucky Press, 1962.

Thornbrough, Gale, ed. *Letter Book of the Indian Agency and Fort Wayne 1809-1815*. Indianapolis, IN: Indiana Historical Society, 1961.

Thwaites, Reuben Gold and Louise Phelps Kellogg. *Documentary History of Dunmore's War*. Madison, WI: Wisconsin Historical Society, 1905.

Thwaites, Reuben Gold and Louise Phelps Kellogg. *Frontier Defense on the Upper Ohio 1777-1778*. Madison, WI: Wisconsin Historical Society, 1912.

Thwaites, Reuben Gold and Louise Phelps Kellogg. *The Revolution on the Upper Ohio 1775-1777*. Madison, WI: Wisconsin Historical Society, 1908.

Van Doren, Mark, ed. *Correspondence of Aaron Burr and his Daughter Theodosia*. New York: Covici, Frieda, Inc., 1929.

Van Every, Dale. *A Company of Heroes: The American Frontier 1775-1783*. New York: Morrow & Co., 1962.

Van Every, Dale. *Forth to the Wilderness*. New York: Morrow & Co., 1961.

Wallace, Paul A. W., ed. *Thirty Thousand Miles with John Heckewelder*. Pittsburgh, PA: University of Pittsburgh Press, 1958.

Wellman, Paul I. *Spawn of Evil*. New York: Doubleday & Co., 1964.

Woehrmann, Paul. *At the Headwaters of the Maumee: A History of the Forts of Fort Wayne*. Indianapolis, IN: Indiana Historical Society, 1971.

Index

OTHER BOOKS BY GARY S. WILLIAMS

Gliding To
A Better Place
Profiles from Ohio's
Territorial Era

back cover:

Who came Gliding to a Better Place?

As the first state to be settled by U. S. citizens, Ohio is the start of our nation's westward movement. Gathered here are the stories of some of the fascinating characters who came. They collectively tell the story of Ohio's Territorial Era. Here, you will read about:

-the Father of our Country's role in westward expansion

-the female frontier scout who was as tough as any man

-the old man who went to the sea again by being the first to sail down the Ohio River

-three Ohio Natives who tried to forge tribal unity in the face of white encroachment

-the U. S. General who tried to undermine Anthony Wayne while being paid by the Spanish government as Agent 13

It's all here: the true stories behind the legends, tales of the courageous and the curmudgeonly, the sagas of the saints and schemers and the soldiers and settlers who came gliding to a better place and carved a new state out of the wilderness.

"Gary Williams shares my fascination for Ohio history. Books like the one he has written are important because they keep Ohio's stories and heroes from fading from our memory."

John Switzer, *Columbus Dispatch* columnist

The
FORTS *of* OHIO
A GUIDE TO
MILITARY STOCKADES

back cover:

*T*he earliest years of Ohio's recorded history were filled with conflict as Americans, Europeans and Native Americans struggled for control of the region. For the white intruders of this era, log forts became the key to survival in this wilderness. The story of these forts is the story of Ohio's beginnings and features some compelling tales.

*A*t which Ohio fort...

- did one of the nation's most famous friendships begin when Lewis met Clark?
- did the officers write a Declaration of Independence that preceded the more famous one by 20 months?
- was a future President arrested for ordering that a civilian be given 50 lashes?
- did the besieged and starving garrison stampede their own relief convoy by firing their guns in celebration?
- was an American general, who was also a spy for Spain, suspected of trying to kill Anthony Wayne?
- did the commander name the post after his eleven-year-old daughter?
- did Tecumseh complain that the Americans "hide behind logs and in the earth like ground hogs"?
- did Commodore Perry send his famous message, "We have met the enemy and they are ours"?

$17.84

ABOUT THE AUTHOR

Gary S. Williams is a lifelong resident of Ohio. A native of Tuscarawas County, his first job was on the archaeological excavation of Fort Laurens, Ohio's only Revolutionary War fort. He has a B.A. in History from Marietta College, a Master's in Library Science from Kent State University, and 25 years experience as a librarian. He is also the author of *Gliding to a Better Place: Profiles from Ohio's Territorial Era* and *The Forts of Ohio: A Guide to Military Stockades*. He lives near Caldwell with his wife, Mary, and children, Owen and Meryl.